tastes of the
mediterranean

The Confident Cooking Promise of Success

Welcome to the world of Confident Cooking,
where recipes are double-tested by our team
of home economists to achieve a high standard
of success—and delicious results every time.

bay books

All recipes are double-tested by our team of home economists. When we test our recipes, we rate them for ease of preparation. The following cookery ratings are on the recipes in this book, making them easy to use and understand.

A single Cooking with Confidence symbol indicates a recipe that is simple and generally quick to make—perfect for beginners.

Two symbols indicate the need for just a little more care and a little more time.

Three symbols indicate special dishes that need more investment in time, care and patience—but the results are worth it.

TEST KITCHEN PERFECTION

You'll never make a wrong move with one of our step-by-step cookbooks. Our team of home economists has tested and refined the recipes so that you can create fabulous food in your own kitchen. Follow our easy instructions and step-by-step photographs and you'll feel like there is a master chef in the kitchen guiding you every step of the way.

IMPORTANT

Those who might be at risk from the effects of salmonella food poisoning (the elderly, pregnant women, young children and those suffering from immune deficiency diseases) should consult their doctor with any concerns about eating raw eggs.

The Publisher thanks: Chief Australia; Breville Holdings Pty Ltd; Kambrook; Bertolli Olive Oil; Southcorp Appliances; Sheldon & Hammond.
Front cover: Grilled calamari with salsa verde, page 25;
Hamad m'rakad (preserved lemons), page 30 and
Insalata caprese (tomato and bocconcini salad), page 51
Inside front cover: Cabbage rolls, page 82
Back cover: Figs in honey syrup, page 101

CONTENTS

Top: Baklava *(Middle eastern nut-filled pastry), page 107* **Bottom left:** *Tuna skewers with Moroccan spices and chermoula, page 64* **Bottom right:** *Roasted fennel and orange salad, page 43*

Healthy Mediterranean cooking

The Mediterranean Sea links Europe, Africa and the Middle East. To follow the Mediterranean model of healthy eating, include in your diet lots of fresh fruit and vegetables, as well as breads, grains and beans. Use olive oil instead of, not as well as, other fats. Eat low to moderate amounts of dairy products. Cook fish and poultry a few times a week and red meat less frequently. Regular exercise is also part of the healthy lifestyle.

The Mediterranean diet

Within the Mediterranean, each country has its own particular cuisine and tends to favour local ingredients. Regions within each country also do this. Indeed, often, areas within regions have their own specialities. So obviously it is just not possible to identify one Mediterranean diet.

The countries in the region have a similar climate and historical influences and this has meant a reliance on similar kinds of foods. The 'Mediterranean diet' has factors which are common in each of the countries: it is low in saturated fats and high in complex carbohydrates and fibre. The diet is based on cereals (bread, pasta, couscous, burghul, rice), vegetables, fruit and legumes, olives, garlic and herbs. Food is grown locally and is eaten at its freshest and best. These foods make up the core of the diet, while foods from animal sources are used less frequently. Limited availability and the cost of red meat mean that it is generally eaten in small quantities and only a few times per month. Fish, poultry and eggs are used a few times a week. Cheese features prominently in the cuisine in some areas but in most areas dairy products are used in low to moderate amounts, perhaps a few times per week. Red wine plays a large part in the Mediterranean diet but is drunk in moderation and almost always during meals. Spirits are imbibed less frequently.

The good oil

Olive oil is the quintessential ingredient that links the diverse Mediterranean cuisines. The flavour, colour and taste varies according to the type of olives used and the climate, soil and area of cultivation. The type and ripeness of the olive influences the colour. Some olive trees are grown to produce olives for eating and some for oil — they are not harvested from the same trees.

Over 30 years ago the Seven Countries Study found that a typical Mediterranean diet resulted in the highest rates of life expectancy. Further studies endorsed by the World Health Organization have shown Mediterranean countries to have the lowest rates of chronic diseases, including coronary heart disease, obesity, diabetes and cancers of the bowel and breast. This applies despite the relative lack of economic wealth in some areas. It seems that

the overwhelming factor in this is a diet low in saturated fats.

We have all become so conditioned to believing that fat is bad that it is difficult for us to believe just how good olive oil is for you. Olive oil is cholesterol-free and is high in oleic acid, a mono-unsaturated fatty acid. Mono-unsaturated fats do not raise blood cholesterol levels the way saturated fats (animal fats and some tropical oils such as palm and coconut oil) do. In fact, the mono-unsaturated fats lower the damaging low-density lipoproteins (LDL) which are responsible for depositing cholesterol in the arteries. This leaves the beneficial high-density lipoproteins (HDL) untouched. Substances present in olive oil also protect LDL cholesterol from oxidation, which is a main feature in the development of coronary artery disease.

Olive oil not only contains large amounts of mono-unsaturated fats (between 55 and 83 per cent) but is also a rich source of antioxidants. Olive oil is also a good source of vitamin E — a powerful antioxidant and disease preventative. Anti-oxidants fight free radicals, elements which can suppress the immune system and may cause heart disease, cancers and ageing.

Why do we need any fat, even if it is olive oil? We need some fat in our diet to help transport essential fat-soluble vitamins A, D, E and K. Also, it makes things taste good. Olive oil helps make the simple Mediterranean foods quite flavoursome. Pasta can be tossed with olive oil and a few other ingredients to give a delicious meal. Olive oil brings out the flavour of other ingredients and is a natural complement to fresh regional produce.

What's in a name?

'Extra virgin olive oil' is unrefined, has the lowest acidity level and is of the highest quality. Extra virgin olive oil is the first extraction of oil from the olives and the extraction is undertaken without heat or chemicals which may alter the oil. Prices vary considerably.

'Virgin olive oil' is similar to extra virgin but has a slightly higher allowable acidity level.

'Olive oil' is from the second extraction and the olives are heated to make the oil thinner and more easily removed.

'Light olive oil' is made from the filtered combination of refined olive oil and small amounts of virgin olive oil. It is not light in kilojoules, just in texture and taste.

As a general rule, you would use olive oil for cooking, whereas the flavour of extra virgin olive oil is often preferred for salad dressings and drizzling on food such as pasta. However, the choice is a personal one. Contrary to popular opinion, olive oil is also suitable for frying as it doesn't break down when heated and also forms a seal around the food, thus minimising fat absorption.

With all the studies that have been done regarding the good health of people in the Mediterranean region, it is still not clear how much can be attributed to diet and what part lifestyle plays in the equation. For example, drinking alcohol is generally done in company and with food, even if it's just the things we know and love as meze, tapas, antipasto or hors d'oeuvres. Olive oil is used instead of, rarely as well as, saturated fats. The diet incorporates plenty of fresh and unprocessed foods, with no hidden saturated fats or refined sugars that are evident in some diets.

Also, we should remember that the traditional Mediterranean lifestyle includes a large amount of physical activity. If you make time for daily exercise, you will be sure to reap the benefits.

Mediterranean pantry

Bocconcini

A fresh, unripened cheese originally made from buffalo milk but now more commonly made from cow milk. It is often referred to as 'baby mozzarella', and is kept in whey to keep it moist. Young fresh mozzarella will keep in the refrigerator for 2–3 weeks. Change the water it is kept in every 2 days.

BOCCONCINI

Burghul

Also known as bulgar or cracked wheat, burghul is a wheat product which has been hulled, parboiled or steamed, then dried and cracked. It is a staple in the Middle East and requires either very little cooking or just soaking. It is available coarse or fine ground.

BURGHUL

Cedro

Also known as citron, cedro originated in north-eastern India before spreading throughout the Middle East and Asia during antiquity. The fruits look like large rough lemons and have a very thick peel and dry flesh with quite a sour flavour. They are now grown especially for their thick peel which is candied. Cedro is available in some speciality shops.

CEDRO

Couscous

A staple food of northern Africa, particularly Morocco and Algeria. Couscous is a processed cereal made from semolina and coated with wheat flour. It is used in much the same way as rice in Asia — as a high-carbohydrate accompaniment to meat and vegetable dishes. Instant couscous is commonly available in supermarkets and cooks in 5 minutes in boiling water.

COUSCOUS

FETA

Feta

A soft white cheese ripened in brine, giving it a characteristic salty taste. Originally made from sheep or goat milk, feta is now most often made with cow milk. Feta takes its name from the word *fetes*, meaning large blocks or slices, which it is cut into before being ripened and stored in brine. It is the best known of all Greek cheeses and can be eaten as an appetizer, cooked or marinated. Available in Bulgarian, German and Australian varieties, which are creamier and slightly salty, and Italian, Greek and Danish varieties which are coarser and more salty.

Haloumi

A salty Middle Eastern cheese made from sheep milk. The name is thought to be one of the few surviving ancient Egyptian words – *ialom*. The curd is heated in whey to boiling, then drained, salted and matured in brine, sometimes with herbs or spices. It is most often grilled or fried to be used in salads or on bread.

Halva

A Middle Eastern sweet with numerous variations, but most generally made from crushed sesame seeds, sugar and glucose or honey. Flavoured with various nuts, fruit, chocolate and spices, halva is made in block form and sold in slices. It is also called halawch.

Kefalotyri cheese

A very hard, pale yellow scalded and cured sheep or goat milk cheese from Greece. The taste and texture are quite similar to the Italian Parmesan cheeses. Kefalotyri has a variety of different uses depending on its age. When young it is used as a table cheese, when six months old it is used in cooking, particularly frying, and when more mature it makes an excellent grating cheese. Parmesan or Pecorino can be substituted.

Lentils

A legume with many varieties originating from the Middle East with red, green and brown being the most common types. Lentils do not have to be soaked before cooking but they should be rinsed to remove any impurities. Lentils are remarkably high in protein (25%) and low in fat, and are therefore an essential part of any vegetarian diet. Green and brown lentils are often mixed together and can be substituted for each other.

Okra

A native of Africa, this green curved pod is very popular in the eastern Mediterranean. It is also called gumbo, a name very popular in the United States, and ladies' fingers. It has a very glutinous texture which can be lessened by soaking in lemon juice and salt water before cooking and is a natural thickening agent. Okra is available both fresh and canned. If using canned, make sure you rinse it well.

Pancetta

An important ingredient in Italian cooking, pancetta is the unsmoked bacon, from the belly of the pig, that has been cured in salt and spices. It is usually sold rolled into a sausage shape and cut into very thin slices. Pancetta can be eaten raw or cooked. If unavailable, bacon can be substituted.

HALOUMI

HALVA

KEFALOTYRI

LENTILS

OKRA

PANCETTA

Parmesan

A hard cow milk cheese widely used in Italy, either grated in dishes or shaved to garnish. Always buy in a chunk and grate it as you need it rather than using ready-grated packet cheese. Parmigiano–reggiano is the most superior, which is reflected in the price, but is well worth it.

Pecorino

A general name for a wide range of Italian cheeses made from sheep milk. More specifically, the name refers to hard, cooked sheep milk cheeses of central Italy and Sardinia. The most famous of these is Pecorino Romano. Pecorino is available mild or sharp, or sometimes with added flavours such as peppercorns. Fresh pecorino is also available.

Polenta

Also known as cornmeal, these ground, dried corn kernels are a staple carbohydrate in northern Italy. It is most often made into a porridge-like mixture with the addition of butter and Parmesan or cooked and left to set, then fried, grilled or baked. Polenta comes in coarse, medium or fine grains.

Pomegranate molasses

Also sold as pomegranate syrup or concentrate. This is the boiled down juice of a sour variety of pomegranate cultivated in Syria and Lebanon. Pomegranate molasses has a sweet and sour flavour and should not be confused with grenadine, a highly sweetened concentrated syrup used in making beverages.

Porcini mushrooms

Known as ceps or boletus mushrooms in France, porcini are wild mushrooms used extensively in Italian and French cooking. While sometimes available fresh, they are most common dried. Dried porcini mushrooms need to be reconstituted by soaking in hot water then rinsed thoroughly to remove any grit. The strained soaking water can also be used to add flavour to the dish. Dried porcini have a strong, meaty flavour and should be used sparingly.

Preserved lemons

A unique flavour popular in northern African dishes, particularly Moroccan tagines. Lemons are packed tightly with salt and sealed in a jar with extra lemon juice and spices such as peppercorns, bay leaves, or even cinnamon and cloves, for up to six weeks. Only the rind is used, so the lemons must be rinsed well and have the pulp and pith removed before use.

Prosciutto

An Italian ham that has been cured by salting, then drying in the air. Aged for 8–10 months, it is then sliced thinly and can be eaten raw or cooked. Prosciutto di Parma is the classic Italian ham and is traditionally served as an antipasto and also used extensively in Italian cooking.

Provolone

A golden yellow mainly southern Italian cheese with a glossy rind, often moulded by hand into a variety of shapes before being hung to mature. While it is young, provolone is mild and delicate and often used as a table cheese. As it matures, the flavour becomes sharper and it can be used for grating. Provolone is often available smoked.

Puy lentils

A tiny, dark green lentil which is regarded as a delicacy in France, their country of origin. They keep their shape and quite a firm texture after cooking and are used most often for salads and hors d'oeuvre. Lentil du Puy are more expensive than other lentils and can be found in speciality shops.

Semolina

The coarse product obtained from the first milling of wheat. Semolina itself is available coarse, medium or fine ground. Often made from durum wheat, it is used in making of pasta, gnocchi and certain puddings or cakes. Semolina is less starchy than other wheat products and results in a lighter texture in the finished products.

Sumac

Dried red berries from the Middle Eastern *Rhus coriaria* or sumac tree containing small, brown, sour seeds. Used mainly in Syria and Lebanon, ground sumac is sprinkled on salads and fish and adds a tangy, citrus flavour. Indeed, it was used as a bitter flavouring in Classical times before the introduction of lemons and is most common today in areas where lemons are still scarce.

SUMAC

SEMOLINA

PUY LENTILS

PROVOLONE

PROSCIUTTO

PARMESAN

PECORINO

POLENTA

POMEGRANATE MOLASSES

PORCINI MUSHROOMS

PRESERVED LEMONS

FROM TAPAS TO MEZE

HUMMUS
(Turkish chickpea dip)

Preparation time: 20 minutes
+ overnight soaking
Total cooking time:
1 hour 15 minutes
Makes 3 cups

220 g (1 cup) dried chickpeas
2 tablespoons tahini
4 garlic cloves, crushed
2 teaspoons ground cumin
80 ml (1/3 cup) lemon juice
3 tablespoons olive oil
large pinch cayenne pepper
extra lemon juice, optional
extra olive oil, to garnish
paprika, to garnish
chopped fresh parsley, to garnish

1 Soak the chickpeas in 1 litre (4 cups) water overnight. Drain and place in a large saucepan with 2 litres (8 cups) fresh water (enough to cover the chickpeas by 5 cm/2 inch). Bring to the boil, then reduce the heat and simmer for 1 hour 15 minutes, or until the chickpeas are very tender. Skim any scum from the surface. Drain well, reserve the cooking liquid and leave until cool enough to handle. Pick over for any loose skins and discard.

2 Process the chickpeas, tahini, garlic, cumin, lemon juice, olive oil, cayenne pepper and 1 1/2 teaspoons salt in a food processor until thick and smooth. With the motor still running, gradually add enough reserved cooking liquid (about 185 ml/3/4 cup) to form a smooth creamy purée. Season with salt or extra lemon juice.

3 Spread onto a flat bowl or plate, drizzle with oil, sprinkle with paprika and scatter the parsley over the top. Serve with pitta bread or pide.

NUTRITION PER SERVE (18)
Protein 1.2 g; Fat 4.7 g; Carbohydrate 1.6 g; Dietary Fibre 0.9 g; Cholesterol 0 mg; 228 kJ (54 Cal)

Pick through the cooled chickpeas to remove any loose skins.

Process the chickpea mixture with the reserved cooking liquid until creamy.

TAPENADE
(Provençal olive, anchovy and caper paste)

Preparation time: 10 minutes
Total cooking time: Nil
Makes 1½ cups

400 g (14 oz) Kalamata olives, pitted
2 garlic cloves, crushed
2 anchovy fillets in oil, drained
2 tablespoons capers in brine, rinsed, squeezed dry
2 teaspoons chopped fresh thyme
2 teaspoons Dijon mustard
1 tablespoon lemon juice
60 ml (¼ cup) olive oil
1 tablespoon brandy, optional

1 Place the Kalamata olives, crushed garlic, anchovies, capers, chopped thyme, Dijon mustard, lemon juice, olive oil and brandy in a food processor and process until smooth. Season to taste with salt and freshly ground black pepper. Spoon into a clean, warm jar, cover with a layer of olive oil, seal and refrigerate for up to 1 week. Serve on bruschetta or with a meze plate.

NUTRITION PER SERVE (9)
Protein 1.3 g; Fat 2.4 g; Carbohydrate 2 g; Dietary Fibre 8.5 g; Cholesterol 0.6 mg; 376 kJ (90 Cal)

COOK'S FILE
Note: When refrigerated, the olive oil may solidify, making it an opaque white colour. This is a property of olive oil and will not affect the flavour of the dish. Simply bring the dish to room temperature before serving and the olive oil with return to a liquid state. The word 'tapenade' comes from the French word tapéno, meaning capers. Tapenade is the famous olive, anchovy and caper spread from Provence.
Hint: To make sure your storage jar is very clean, preheat the oven to 120°C (250°F/Gas ½). Wash the jar and lid thoroughly in hot soapy water (or preferably in a dishwasher) and rinse well with hot water. Put the jar on a baking tray and place in the oven for 20 minutes, or until fully dry and you are ready to use it. Do not dry the jar or lid with a tea towel.

Use an olive pitter or small sharp knife to remove the stones from the olives.

Process all the ingredients in a food processor until smooth.

PESTO
(Italian basil sauce)

Preparation time: 10 minutes
Total cooking time: 2 minutes
Makes 1 cup

50 g (1/3 cup) pine nuts
50 g (1 cup) small fresh basil leaves
2 garlic cloves, crushed

1/2 teaspoon sea salt
125 ml (1/2 cup) olive oil
30 g (1/3 cup) Parmesan cheese, finely grated
20 g (1/2 cup) pecorino cheese, finely grated

1 Preheat the oven to 180°C (350°F/ Gas 4). Spread the pine nuts on a baking tray and bake for 2 minutes, or until lightly golden. Cool.
2 Place the pine nuts, basil, garlic, salt and oil in a food processor and process until smooth. Transfer to a bowl and stir in the cheeses. Serve with a meze plate, pasta, meat or soup.

NUTRITION PER SERVE (6)
Protein 4 g; Fat 28 g; Carbohydrate 0.5 g; Dietary Fibre 0.6 g; Cholesterol 7.6 mg; 1118 kJ (267 Cal)

COOK'S FILE
Note: Pesto is a famous Italian sauce, served with dishes like chicken and fish.

Bake the pine nuts in a moderate oven until lightly golden.

Process the pine nuts, basil, garlic, sea salt and oil until smooth.

Stir the Parmesan and pecorino into the basil mixture.

SKORDALIA
(Greek garlic sauce)

Preparation time: 15 minutes
Total cooking time: 10 minutes
Makes 2 cups

500 g (1 lb 2 oz) floury potatoes,
 peeled and cut into 2 cm (3/4 inch)
 cubes (see Notes)
5 garlic cloves, crushed
ground white pepper

185 ml (3/4 cup) olive oil
2 tablespoons white vinegar

1 Bring a saucepan of water to the
boil, add the potato and cook for
10 minutes, or until very soft.
2 Drain the potato and mash until
quite smooth. Stir in the garlic,
1 teaspoon salt and a pinch of white
pepper. Gradually pour in the oil,
mixing well with a wooden spoon. Add
the vinegar and season, if needed.
Serve with crusty bread or crackers,
or with grilled meat, fish or chicken.

NUTRITION PER SERVE (12)
Protein 1 g; Fat 14.8 g; Carbohydrate 5.6 g;
Dietary Fibre 0.9 g; Cholesterol 0 mg;
662 kJ (158 Cal)

COOK'S FILE
Notes: Use King Edward, russet or
pontiac potatoes.
Do not make skordalia with a food
processor—the processing will turn the
potato into a gluey mess.
Storage: Skordalia will keep in an airtight
container for up to 2–3 days in the
fridge. The potato will absorb the salt so
check the seasoning before serving.

*Boil the potato in a large saucepan of
lightly salted water until very soft.*

*Drain the potato and then mash with a
potato masher until smooth.*

*Gradually add the oil to the potato
mixture, mixing well.*

TZATZIKI
(Greek cucumber and yoghurt dip)

Preparation time: 10 minutes
+ 15 minutes standing
Total cooking time: Nil
Makes 2 cups

2 Lebanese (short) cucumbers
(about 300 g/10½ oz)
400 g (14 oz) Greek-style plain yoghurt
4 garlic cloves, crushed
3 tablespoons finely chopped fresh
mint, plus extra to garnish
1 tablespoon lemon juice

1   Cut the cucumbers in half lengthways, scoop out the seeds and discard. Leave the skin on and coarsely grate the cucumber into a small colander. Sprinkle with salt and leave over a large bowl for 15 minutes to drain off any bitter juices.
2   Meanwhile, place the Greek-style yoghurt, crushed garlic, mint and lemon juice in a bowl, and stir until well combined.
3   Rinse the cucumber under cold water then, taking small handfuls, squeeze out any excess moisture. Combine the grated cucumber with the yoghurt mixture, then season to taste with salt and freshly ground

black pepper. Serve immediately or refrigerate until ready to serve, garnished with the extra mint.

NUTRITION PER SERVE (12)
Protein 1.6 g; Fat 1.2 g; Carbohydrate 2.3 g; Dietary Fibre 0.5 g; Cholesterol 5.3 mg; 119 kJ (28 Cal)

COOK'S FILE
Note: Tzatziki is often served as a dip with flatbread or Turkish pide but is also suitable to serve as a sauce to accompany seafood and meat.
Storage: Tzatziki will keep in an airtight container in the refrigerator for 2–3 days.

Cut the cucumbers in half and scoop out the seeds with a teaspoon.

Mix the yoghurt, garlic, mint and lemon juice together.

Squeeze the grated cucumber to remove any excess moisture.

MARINATED FETA

Preparation time: 10 minutes
 + 24 hours soaking
 + 1 week maturing
Total cooking time: Nil
Fills a 750 ml (3 cup) jar

4 garlic cloves, peeled
125 ml (½ cup) lemon juice
400 g (14 oz) good-quality soft feta
6 fresh thyme sprigs
2 fresh bay leaves, lightly crushed
½ teaspoon black peppercorns
up to 375 ml (1½ cups) good-quality
 olive oil

1 Soak the garlic cloves in the lemon juice for 24 hours. Drain and pat dry with paper towels. Drain the feta and cut into 2 cm (¾ inch) cubes. Layer the feta, thyme, garlic, bay leaves and peppercorns in a 750 ml (3 cup) jar with a tight-fitting lid.

2 Fill the jar with oil to completely cover. Seal the jar and refrigerate for 1 week before using. Refrigerate for up to 3 weeks after opening.

NUTRITION PER SERVE (6)
Protein 12 g; Fat 34.5 g; Carbohydrate 1.0 g; Dietary Fibre 0.5 g; Cholesterol 46 mg; 1515 kJ (360 Cal)

COOK'S FILE
Storage: The oil may solidify in the fridge. Bring to room temperature for serving. Chill after opening; use within 2 weeks.

Drain the soft feta well and cut into 2 cm (¾ inch) cubes.

Fill the jar with good-quality olive oil to cover the contents.

14

TARAMOSALATA
(Greek fish roe purée)

Preparation time: 10 minutes
  + 10 minutes soaking
Total cooking time: Nil
Makes 1 1/2 cups

5 slices white bread, crusts removed
80 ml (1/3 cup) milk
100 g (3 1/2 oz) can tarama (mullet roe)
1 egg yolk

1/2 small onion, grated
1 garlic clove, crushed
2 tablespoons lemon juice
80 ml (1/3 cup) olive oil
pinch ground white pepper

1 Soak the bread in the milk for 10 minutes. Press in a strainer to extract any excess milk, then place in a food processor with the tarama, egg yolk, onion and garlic. Process for 30 seconds, or until smooth, then add 1 tablespoon lemon juice.
2 With the motor running, slowly pour in the olive oil. The mixture should be smooth and of a dipping consistency. Add the remaining lemon juice and a pinch of white pepper. If the dip tastes too salty, add another piece of bread.

NUTRITION PER SERVE (9)
Protein 3.8 g; Fat 10.4 g; Carbohydrate 8.3 g; Dietary Fibre 0.6 g; Cholesterol 57 mg; 596 kJ (142 Cal)

COOK'S FILE
Variation: Try smoked cod's roe instead of the mullet roe.

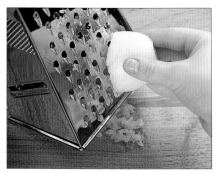

Using a cheese grater, grate half a small onion.

Press the soaked bread pieces in a strainer to extract any excess milk.

Process the bread, tarama, egg yolk, onion and garlic until smooth.

BABA GHANNOUJ
(Turkish eggplant dip)

Preparation time: 20 minutes
+ 30 minutes cooling
Total cooking time: 50 minutes
Makes 1¾ cups

2 eggplants (aubergines)
   (1 kg/1 lb 2 oz)
3 garlic cloves, crushed
½ teaspoon ground cumin
80 ml (⅓ cup) lemon juice
2 tablespoons tahini
pinch cayenne pepper
1½ tablespoons olive oil
1 tablespoon finely chopped fresh
   flat-leaf (Italian) parsley
black olives, to garnish

1 Preheat the oven to 200°C (400°F/
Gas 6). Pierce the eggplants several
times with a fork, then cook over an
open flame for about 5 minutes, or
until the skin is black and blistering,
then place in a roasting tin and bake
for 40–45 minutes, or until the
eggplants are very soft and wrinkled.
Place in a colander over a bowl to
drain off any bitter juices and leave
to stand for 30 minutes, or until cool.
2 Carefully peel the skin from the
eggplant, chop the flesh and place
in a food processor with the garlic,
cumin, lemon, tahini, cayenne and
olive oil. Process until smooth and
creamy. Alternatively, use a potato
masher or fork. Season to taste with
salt and stir in the parsley. Spread
onto a flat bowl or plate and garnish
with the olives. Serve with flatbread
or pide.

NUTRITION PER SERVE (10)
Protein 1.8 g; Fat 5 g; Carbohydrate 3 g;
Dietary Fibre 3 g; Cholesterol 0 mg;
269 kJ (64 Cal)

COOK'S FILE
Note: If you prefer, you can simply roast
the eggplant in a roasting tin in a 200°C
(400°F/Gas 6) oven for 1 hour, or until
very soft and wrinkled. The name baba
ghannouj is roughly translated as
'poor man's caviar'.

Carefully peel the skin away from the baked eggplant.

Process the eggplant, garlic, cumin, lemon, tahini, cayenne and olive oil.

BOREK
(Turkish filo parcels)

Preparation time: 1 hour
Total cooking time: 20 minutes
Makes 24

400 g (14 oz) soft feta
2 eggs, lightly beaten
25 g (³/4 cup) chopped fresh flat-leaf
    (Italian) parsley
375 g (13 oz) filo pastry
80 ml (¹/3 cup) good-quality olive oil

1 Preheat the oven to 180°C (350°F/ Gas 4). Lightly grease a baking tray. Crumble the feta into a large bowl using a fork or your fingers. Mix in the eggs and parsley, and season with black pepper.
2 Lightly brush 4 sheets of pastry with olive oil and place the sheets on top of each other. Cut the pastry into four 7 cm (2³/4 inch) strips.
3 Place 2 rounded teaspoons of the feta mixture in one corner of each strip and fold diagonally, creating a triangle pillow effect. Place on the baking tray, seam-side-down,

and brush the top with olive oil. Repeat with the remaining pastry and filling to make 24 boreks. Discard any leftover pastry. Bake for 20 minutes, or until golden. Serve as part of a large meze plate.

NUTRITION PER BOREK
Protein 5 g; Fat 7.8 g; Carbohydrate 8.5 g; Dietary Fibre 0 g; Cholesterol 26 mg; 522 kJ (125 Cal)

COOK'S FILE
Note: Keep the filo pastry covered with a damp tea towel when you are not using it so it doesn't dry out.

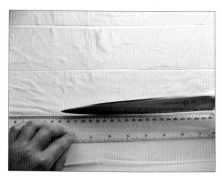

Cut the lightly oiled filo pastry layers into four strips.

Place some feta mixture in the corner of each pastry strip.

Fold the pastry diagonally, creating a triangle pillow effect.

BRUSCHETTA

To make basic bruschetta, cut a crusty Italian loaf into twelve 1.5 cm (3/4 inch) diagonal slices. Toast or grill (broil) the slices until golden. Bruise 2 garlic cloves with the flat of a knife, peel and rub the cloves over both sides of the hot bread. Drizzle the tops with a little extra virgin olive oil and finish with one of these delicious toppings.

ANCHOVY, TOMATO AND OREGANO

Deseed and roughly chop 3 vine-ripened tomatoes and mix with 1 small chopped red onion, a 90 g (3³/4 oz) jar drained, minced anchovy fillets and 2 tablespoons olive oil. Spoon some of the mixture onto each bruschetta. Drizzle with extra virgin olive oil, and garnish with chopped fresh oregano and freshly ground black pepper.

BLACK OLIVE PATE, ROCKET AND FETA

Place 100 g (3¹/2 oz) trimmed baby rocket leaves, 75 g (2¹/2 oz) crumbled Greek feta and 2 tablespoons olive oil in a bowl, and mix together well. Spread 2 teaspoons of black olive pâté onto each bruschetta slice and top with the feta mixture. Drizzle with extra virgin olive oil and season with sea salt and freshly ground black pepper.

SUN-DRIED TOMATO PESTO, ARTICHOKE AND BOCCONCINI

Spread 1 teaspoon of good-quality sun-dried (sun-blushed) tomato pesto onto each slice of bruschetta. Slice 12 (360 g/12¹/4 oz) bocconcini and place on top of the pesto. Chop 55 g (2 oz) drained marinated artichoke hearts in oil and place over the bocconcini slices. Sprinkle with finely chopped fresh flat-leaf (Italian) parsley.

PESTO, RED CAPSICUM AND PARMESAN

Cut 3 red capsicums (peppers) into large flattish pieces and remove the seeds and membrane. Cook the capsicum pieces, skin-side-up, under a hot grill (broiler) until the skin blackens and blisters. Place in a plastic bag and leave to cool. When cool enough to handle, peel away the skin. Discard the skin and cut the flesh into 1 cm ($^1/_2$ inch) strips. Spread 2 teaspoons good-quality basil pesto onto each slice of the bruschetta. Top with the capsicum strips and 50 g ($^1/_2$ cup) fresh Parmesan shards. Drizzle with extra virgin olive oil and season with sea salt and ground black pepper.

MUSHROOM AND GOAT'S CHEESE

Preheat the oven to 180°C (350°F/ Gas 4). Mix 125 ml ($^1/_2$ cup) olive oil with 3 chopped garlic cloves, 2 tablespoons chopped fresh flat-leaf (Italian) parsley and 1 tablespoon dry sherry. Place 6 large field mushrooms on a foil-lined baking tray and spoon on all but 2 tablespoons of mixture. Bake for 20 minutes, or until soft. Mix 150 g ($5^1/_2$ oz) goat's cheese with 1 teaspoon chopped fresh thyme, then spread over the bruschetta. Warm the remaining oil mixture. Cut the mushrooms in half and place one half on each bruschetta. Drizzle with the remaining oil. Season with sea salt and ground black pepper.

PAN CON TOMATE

Place 4 seeded and roughly chopped large vine-ripened tomatoes, 15 g ($^1/_2$ cup) roughly torn fresh basil leaves, 2 tablespoons olive oil and $^1/_2$ teaspoon caster (superfine) sugar in a bowl and mix together well. Season wth plenty of sea salt and freshly ground black pepper and set the mixture aside for 10–15 minutes so the flavours have time to infuse and develop. Cut a ripe vine-ripened tomato in half and rub it on the oiled side of the slices of bruschetta, squeezing the tomato to extract as much of the liquid as possible. Carefully spoon 2 tablespoons of the tomato mixture onto each slice of bruschetta and serve immediately.

Left to right: Anchovy, tomato and oregano bruschetta; Black olive pâté, rocket and feta bruschetta; Sun-dried tomato pesto, artichoke and bocconcini bruschetta; Pesto, red capsicum and Parmesan bruschetta; Mushroom and goat's cheese bruschetta; Pan con tomate.

TABBOULEH
(Lebanese parsley and burghul salad)

Preparation time: 20 minutes
+ 1 hour 30 minutes soaking
+ 30 minutes drying
Total cooking time: Nil
Serves 6

130 g (^{3}/4 cup) burghul (bulgar)
3 ripe tomatoes (300 g/10^1/2 oz)
1 telegraph cucumber
4 spring onions (scallions), sliced
120 g (4 cups) chopped fresh
flat-leaf (Italian) parsley
10 g (^{1}/2 cup) fresh mint, chopped

Dressing
80 ml (^{1}/3 cup) lemon juice
60 ml (^{1}/4 cup) olive oil
1 tablespoon extra virgin olive oil

1 Place the burghul in a bowl, cover with 500 ml (2 cups) water and leave for 1 hour 30 minutes.
2 Cut the tomatoes in half, squeeze gently to remove any excess seeds and cut into 1 cm (^{1}/2 inch) cubes. Cut the cucumber in half lengthways, remove the seeds with a teaspoon and cut the flesh into 1 cm (^{1}/2 inch) cubes.
3 To make the dressing, whisk the lemon juice and 1^1/2 teaspoons salt in a bowl until well combined. Season well with freshly ground black pepper and slowly whisk in the olive oil and extra virgin olive oil.
4 Drain the burghul and squeeze out any excess water. Spread the burghul on a clean tea towel or paper towels and leave to dry for 30 minutes. Place the burghul in a large salad bowl, add the tomato, cucumber, spring onion and herbs, and toss to combine. Pour the dressing over the salad and toss until evenly coated. Delicious served with bread.

NUTRITION PER SERVE
Protein 4 g; Fat 13 g; Carbohydrate 22 g; Dietary Fibre 3.5 g; Cholesterol 0 mg; 950 kJ (227 Cal)

Whisk the olive oil and extra virgin olive oil into the lemon juice.

Drain the burghul and squeeze out any excess water.

Toss the salad ingredients together before adding the dressing.

LABNEH MAKBUR
(Marinated yoghurt cheese balls)

Preparation time: 35 minutes
+ 3 days draining
+ 3 hours refrigeration
Total cooking time: Nil
Makes 18 balls

1.5 kg (3 lb 5 oz) plain yoghurt
2 clean 50 x 50 cm (20 x 20 inch)
   muslin squares
2 fresh bay leaves
3 sprigs fresh thyme
2 sprigs fresh oregano
500 ml (2 cups) good-quality olive oil

1 Place the yoghurt in a bowl with 2 teaspoons salt and mix well. Put the muslin squares one on top of the other and place the yoghurt mixture in the centre. Gather up the corners and tie securely with string; suspend over a bowl. Refrigerate and leave to drain for 3 days.
2 Once drained, the yoghurt will become the texture and consistency of ricotta cheese. Remove from the cloth, and place in a bowl.
3 Roll a tablespoon of the mixture into a ball and place on a large tray. Repeat with the remaining mixture to make 18 balls. Cover and refrigerate for 3 hours, or until quite firm.
4 Place the balls in a clean, dry

1 litre (4 cup) glass jar with the bay leaves, thyme and oregano sprigs. Fill the jar with the olive oil. Seal and refrigerate for up to 1 week. Return to room temperature for serving.

NUTRITION PER BALL
Protein 4 g; Fat 9 g; Carbohydrate 4 g; Dietary Fibre 0 g; Cholesterol 13.5 mg; 490 kJ (115 Cal)

COOK'S FILE
Note: This dish is traditionally served at breakfast or as an appetizer.
Hint: Leave the bay leaves, thyme and oregano out of the fridge for 24 hours before use to remove excess moisture.

Place the yoghurt mixture in the muslin, gather up the corners and tie securely.

Roll the yoghurt mixture into balls and place on a large tray.

Place the labneh in the jar with the herbs and pour in the olive oil.

SAGANAKI HALOUMI
(Fried haloumi cheese)

Preparation time: 5 minutes
Total cooking time: 2 minutes
Serves 6

400 g (14 oz) haloumi cheese
80 ml (1/3 cup) olive oil
2 tablespoons lemon juice

1 Pat the haloumi dry with paper
towels; cut into 1 cm (1/2 inch) slices.
2 Pour the oil into a large frying
pan to a depth of 5 mm (1/4 inch)
and heat over medium-high heat.
Cook the cheese in a single layer for
1 minute each side, or until golden.
Remove from the heat and pour on

the lemon juice. Season with pepper
and serve immediately as part of a
meze spread. Serve with crusty bread.

NUTRITION PER SERVE
Protein 14 g; Fat 24 g; Carbohydrate 1.5 g;
Dietary Fibre 0 g; Cholesterol 35 mg;
1156 kJ (276 Cal)

*Cook the haloumi slices in olive oil until
golden on both sides.*

COOK'S FILE:
Note: Saganaki means a two-handled
frying pan. This dish is traditionally
served in the saganaki at the table.
It is served with bread that has been
dipped into the leftover lemon-flavoured
oil in the pan.

*Remove the pan from the heat and pour
on the lemon juice.*

PATATAS BRAVAS
(Spanish crisp potatoes in spicy tomato sauce)

Preparation time: 15 minutes
Total cooking time: 1 hour
Serves 6

1 kg (2 lb 4 oz) desiree potatoes
olive oil, for deep-frying
500 g (1 lb 2 oz) ripe Roma (plum)
   tomatoes
2 tablespoons olive oil, extra
¼ red onion, finely chopped
2 garlic cloves, crushed
3 teaspoons paprika
¼ teaspoon cayenne pepper
1 bay leaf
1 teaspoon sugar
1 tablespoon chopped fresh
   flat-leaf (Italian) parsley

1 Peel the potatoes and cut into 2 cm (³/4 inch) cubes. Rinse then drain well and pat completely dry. Fill a deep fryer or large heavy-based saucepan one third full of oil and heat to 180°C (350°F), or until a cube of bread dropped in the oil browns in 15 seconds. Cook the potato in batches for 10 minutes, or until golden. Drain on crumpled paper towels. Do not discard the oil.
2 Score a cross in the base of each tomato. Place in a bowl of boiling water for 1 minute, then plunge into cold water and peel the skin away from the cross. Chop the flesh.
3 Heat the extra oil in a saucepan and cook the onion over medium heat for 3 minutes, or until soft and light gold. Add the garlic and spices and cook for 1–2 minutes, or until fragrant.
4 Add the tomato, bay leaf, sugar and 100 ml (3½ fl oz) water. Cook, stirring occasionally, for 20 minutes, or until thick and pulpy. Cool slightly and remove the bay leaf. Place the sauce in a food processor and process until smooth, adding a little water if necessary. Prior to serving, return the sauce to the pan and simmer over low heat for 2 minutes, or until heated through. Season well.
5 Reheat the oil to 180°C (350°F), or until a cube of bread dropped in

the oil browns in 15 seconds. Recook the potato in batches for 2 minutes, or until very crisp and golden. Drain on paper towels. This second frying makes the potato extra crispy and stops the sauce soaking in at once. Serve on a platter and pour the sauce over the top. Garnish with parsley.

NUTRITION PER SERVE
Protein 5 g; Fat 13 g; Carbohydrate 25 g; Dietary Fibre 4 g; Cholesterol 0 mg; 1000 kJ (239 Cal)

Deep-fry the potato cubes in olive oil until golden.

Cook the tomato mixture for 20 minutes, or until thick and pulpy.

Deep-fry the potato cubes again, until very crispy and golden.

ELIOPSOMO
(Greek olive bread)

Preparation time: 30 minutes
+ 2 hour 30 minutes rising
Total cooking time: 35 minutes
Makes 1 loaf

375 g (3 cups) plain (all-purpose) flour
7 g (¼ oz) sachet dry yeast
2 teaspoons sugar
2 tablespoons olive oil
110 g (3¾ oz) Kalamata olives, pitted, halved
2 teaspoons plain (all-purpose) flour, extra
1 small sprig fresh oregano, leaves removed and torn into small pieces
olive oil, to glaze

1 Place a third of the flour in a large bowl and stir in 1 teaspoon salt. Place the yeast, sugar and 250 ml (1 cup) warm water in a small bowl, and mix well. Add to the flour and stir to make a thin, lumpy paste. Cover with a tea towel. Leave in a warm place for 45 minutes, or until doubled in size.
2 Stir in the remaining flour, the oil and 125 ml (½ cup) warm water. Mix with a wooden spoon until a rough dough forms. Transfer to a lightly floured work surface and knead for 10–12 minutes, incorporating as little extra flour as possible to keep the dough soft and moist, but not sticky. Form into a ball. Oil a clean large bowl and roll the dough around in it to lightly coat in the oil. Cut a cross on top, cover the bowl with a tea towel and set aside in a warm place for 1 hour, or until doubled in size.
3 Grease a baking tray and dust with flour. Punch down the dough on a

lightly floured surface. Roll out to a 30 cm x 25 cm x 1 cm (12 inch x 10 inch x ½ inch) rectangle. Squeeze any excess liquid from the olives and toss to coat in the extra flour. Scatter over the dough and top with the oregano. Roll up tightly lengthways, pressing firmly to expel any air pockets. Press the ends together to form an oval loaf 25 cm (10 inch) long. Transfer to the tray, seam-side-down. Slide the tray into a large

plastic bag and leave in a warm place for 45 minutes, or until doubled.
4 Preheat the oven to 220°C (425°F/ Gas 7). Brush the top of the loaf with oil and bake for 30 minutes. Reduce the heat to 180°C (350°F/Gas 4) and bake for a further 5 minutes. Cool on a wire rack. Serve warm or cold.

NUTRITION PER LOAF
Protein 46 g; Fat 47 g; Carbohydrate 296 g; Dietary Fibre 20 g; Cholesterol 0 mg; 7532 kJ (1799 Cal)

Leave the yeast mixture in a warm place until doubled in size.

Scatter the olives and oregano over the dough and roll up lengthways.

When the dough has doubled, remove from the bag.

GRILLED CALAMARI WITH SALSA VERDE

Preparation time: 30 minutes
  + 30 minutes marinating
Total cooking time: 15 minutes
Serves 4

1 kg (2 lb 4 oz) calamari (squid)
250 ml (1 cup) olive oil
2 tablespoons lemon juice
2 garlic cloves, crushed
2 tablespoons chopped fresh oregano
2 tablespoons chopped fresh flat-leaf
   (Italian) parsley
6 lemon wedges

Salsa verde
2 anchovy fillets, drained
1 tablespoon capers
1 garlic clove, crushed
2 tablespoons chopped fresh flat-leaf
   (Italian) parsley
2 tablespoons olive oil

1 To clean the calamari, hold onto the hood and gently pull the tentacles away from the head. Cut out the beak and discard with any intestines still attached to the tentacles. Rinse the tentacles in cold running water, pat dry and cut into 5 cm (2 inch) lengths. Place in a bowl. Clean out the hood cavity and remove the transparent backbone. Under cold running water, pull away the skin, rinse and dry well. Cut into 1 cm (½ inch) rings and place in the bowl with the tentacles. Add the oil, lemon juice, garlic and oregano and toss to coat the calamari. Refrigerate for 30 minutes.
2 To make the salsa verde, crush the anchovy fillets in a mortar and pestle or in a bowl with a wooden spoon.

Rinse the capers and dry with paper towels. Chop the capers very finely and add to the anchovies. Add the garlic and parsley, then slowly stir in the olive oil. Season with black pepper and salt, if necessary (the anchovies may be very salty). Mix well.
3 Drain the calamari and cook on a hot barbecue or grill (griddle) in

4 batches for 1–2 minutes each side, basting with the marinade. To serve, sprinkle with salt, pepper and fresh parsley, and serve with the salsa verde and lemon wedges.

NUTRITION PER SERVE
Protein 42.5 g; Fat 72 g; Carbohydrate 0.5 g; Dietary Fibre 0.5 g; Cholesterol 499 mg; 3404 kJ (813 Cal)

Hold the calamari and gently pull the tentacles away from the head.

Combine the anchovies, capers, garlic and parsley.

Cook the calamari in batches on a hot barbecue or grill.

AIOLI WITH CRUDITES
(French garlic mayonnaise with blanched vegetables)

Preparation time: 15 minutes
Total cooking time: 1 minute
Serves 4

4 garlic cloves, crushed
2 egg yolks
300 ml (10½ fl oz) light olive or
    vegetable oil
1 tablespoon lemon juice
pinch ground white pepper
12 asparagus spears, trimmed
26 radishes, trimmed
½ telegraph cucumber, seeded,
    halved and cut into batons
1 head witlof (Belgian endive), leaves
    separated

1 Place the garlic, egg yolks and a pinch of salt in the bowl of a food processor. Process for 10 seconds.
2 With the motor running, add the oil in a thin, slow stream. The mixture will start to thicken. When this happens, add the oil a little faster. Process until all the oil is incorporated and the mayonnaise is thick and creamy. Transfer to a bowl, stir in the lemon juice and pepper.
3 Bring a saucepan of water to the boil, add the asparagus and cook for 1 minute, then plunge into a bowl of iced water. Arrange the asparagus, radish, cucumber and witlof on a platter around the bowl of aïoli. Aïoli can also be used as a sandwich spread or as a sauce for chicken or fish.

NUTRITION PER SERVE
Protein 3 g; Fat 74 g; Carbohydrate 1.5 g; Dietary Fibre 2 g; Cholesterol 90 mg; 28807 kJ (670 Cal)

COOK'S FILE
Note: Should the mayonnaise start to curdle, beat in 1–2 teaspoons boiling water. If this fails, put another egg yolk in a clean bowl and very slowly whisk in the curdled mixture, one drop at a time, then continue as above.
Hint: For best results, make sure all the ingredients are at room temperature when making this recipe.

Seed the cucumbers, then halve widthways and cut into batons.

Stir the lemon juice into the thick and creamy mayonnaise.

Refresh the asparagus spears by plunging into a bowl of iced water.

FALAFEL
(Deep-fried chickpea balls)

Preparation time: 35 minutes
+ 48 hours soaking
+ 50 minutes standing
Total cooking time: 10 minutes
Makes 30

150 g (1 cup) dried split broad (fava)
    beans (see Note)
220 g (1 cup) dried chickpeas
1 onion, roughly chopped
6 garlic cloves, roughly chopped
2 teaspoons ground coriander
1 tablespoon ground cumin
15 g (½ cup) chopped fresh flat-leaf
    (Italian) parsley
¼ teaspoon chilli powder
½ teaspoon bicarbonate of soda
3 tablespoons chopped fresh
    coriander (cilantro) leaves
light oil, for deep-frying

1 Place the broad beans in a large bowl, cover with 750 ml (3 cups) water and leave to soak for 48 hours. (Drain the beans, rinse and cover with fresh water once or twice.)
2 Place the chickpeas in a large bowl, cover with 750 ml (3 cups) water and soak for 12 hours.
3 Drain the beans and chickpeas and pat dry with paper towels. Process in a food processor with the onion and garlic until smooth.
4 Add the ground coriander, cumin, parsley, chilli powder, bicarbonate of soda and fresh coriander. Season with salt and freshly ground black pepper, and mix until well combined. Transfer to a large bowl, knead and leave for 30 minutes.
5 Shape tablespoons of the mixture into balls, flatten slightly, place on a tray and leave for 20 minutes.
6 Fill a deep, heavy-based saucepan one third full of oil and heat to 180°C (350°F), or until a cube of bread browns in 15 seconds. Cook the

falafel in batches for 1–2 minutes, or until golden. Drain on paper towels. Serve hot or cold with hummus, baba ghannouj and pitta bread.

NUTRITION PER FALAFEL
Protein 1.5 g; Fat 2.5 g; Carbohydrate 2.5 g; Dietary Fibre 1.5 g; Cholesterol 0 mg; 101 kJ (24 Cal)

COOK'S FILE
Note: Split broad beans are available from specialist food stores. It is best to get the split broad beans as they are already skinned. If whole broad beans are used they will need to be skinned after soaking. To do this, firmly squeeze each bean to allow the skin to pop off, or slice the skin with your fingernail and then peel it off.

Process the soaked and drained broad beans and chickpeas until very smooth.

Shape the mixture into balls, then flatten slightly into rounds.

27

KIYMALI PIDE
(Turkish flatbread)

Preparation time: 30 minutes
  + 2 hours 20 minutes rising
Total cooking time: 20 minutes
Makes 6

½ teaspoon sugar
2 x 7 g (¼ oz) sachets dry yeast
60 g (½ cup) plain (all-purpose) flour
435 g (3½ cups) bread flour
  (see Note)
60 ml (¼ cup) olive oil
1 egg, lightly beaten with 60 ml
  (¼ cup) water
nigella or sesame seeds, to sprinkle

1 Place the sugar in a large bowl with 125 ml (½ cup) warm water and stir until dissolved. Stir in the yeast, then add the plain flour and mix until smooth. Cover with a plate and leave for 30 minutes, or until frothy and trebled in size.
2 Place the bread flour in a bowl with 1 teaspoon salt. Add the olive oil, 270 ml (9½ fl oz) warm water and the yeast mixture. Mix to a loose dough. Turn out onto a lightly floured surface and knead for 15 minutes. Add minimal flour as the dough needs to be very soft and moist.
3 Shape into a ball and place in a large oiled bowl. Cover with a clean tea towel and leave in a warm place for 1 hour, or until trebled in size. Punch down, divide into 6 equal portions and lightly shape into smooth balls, kneading as little as possible. Place these apart on a tray and place the tray in a plastic bag. Leave for 10 minutes.
4 Sprinkle a large baking tray with

flour. Roll out three balls of dough to a 15 cm (6 inch) circle and place on the baking tray, leaving room for spreading. Cover the dough with a tea towel and rest for 20 minutes. Preheat the oven to 230°C (450°F/ Gas 8) and place another baking tray on the centre rack.
5 Indent the surface of the dough with your finger. Brush with the egg mixture and sprinkle with seeds. Place the tray on the heated tray and bake for 8–10 minutes, or until puffed and golden. Wrap in a tea towel to

soften the crusts while cooling. Repeat with the remaining dough.

NUTRITION PER PIDE
Protein 11 g; Fat 11 g; Carbohydrate 61 g; Dietary Fibre 3.5 g; Cholesterol 30 mg; 1633 kJ (390 Cal)

COOK'S FILE
Note: If bread flour is unavailable, use plain flour. Start by adding half the water in step 2 then gradually add the rest until a loose, soft dough forms. Bread flour requires more water. The holey texture of pide will be lessened using plain flour.

Leave the flour and yeast mixture to stand until frothy and trebled in size.

Knead the dough for 15 minutes, or until soft and moist.

Indent the surface of the dough with your finger.

KALAMARIA TOURSI
(Pickled calamari)

Preparation time: 25 minutes
  + 1 week maturing
Total cooking time: 5 minutes
Serves 4

1 kg (2 lb 4 oz) small calamari (squid)
4 fresh bay leaves
4 sprigs fresh oregano
10 whole black peppercorns
2 teaspoons coriander seeds
1 small red chilli, halved, seeded
625 ml (2 1/2 cups) good-quality
    white wine vinegar
2–3 tablespoons olive oil

1 Grasp the calamari body in one hand and the head and tentacles in the other and pull apart to separate. Cut the tentacles from the head by cutting below the eyes. Discard the head. Push out the beak and discard. Pull the quill from inside the body and discard. Pull away the skin under cold running water. The flaps can be used. Cut the hood into 7 mm (3/8 inch) rings.

2 Place 2 litres (8 cups) water and 1 bay leaf in a large saucepan. Bring to the boil and add the calamari and 1 teaspoon salt. Reduce the heat and simmer for 5 minutes. Drain and dry well.

3 Pack the calamari into a very clean, dry 500 ml (2 cup) jar with a sealing lid. Add the oregano, peppercorns, coriander seeds, chilli and remaining bay leaves. Cover completely with the vinegar then gently pour in enough olive oil to cover by 2 cm (3/4 inch). Seal and refrigerate for 1 week before opening.

NUTRITION PER SERVE
Protein 42 g; Fat 17 g; Carbohydrate 0 g;
Dietary Fibre 0 g; Cholesterol 498 mg;
1450 kJ (345 Cal)

COOK'S FILE
Note: To make sure your storage jar is very clean, wash it, and the lid, in hot soapy water, or in a dishwasher, rinse well in hot water and then dry in a 120°C (250°F/Gas 1/2) oven for 20 minutes, or until you are ready to use them. Don't dry with a tea towel.

Push the beak up and out of the body, and then discard it.

Remove the transparent quill from the body of the calamari.

Gently simmer the calamari rings for 5 minutes, then drain.

Pour enough oil into the jar to cover all the ingredients by 2 cm (3/4 inch).

HAMAD M'RAKAD
(Preserved lemons)

Preparation time: 1 hour
+ 6 weeks standing
Total cooking time: Nil
Fills a 2 litre (8 cup) jar

8–12 small thin-skinned lemons
315 g (1 cup) rock salt
500 ml (2 cups) lemon juice
(8–10 lemons)
½ teaspoon black peppercorns
1 bay leaf
1 tablespoon olive oil

1 Scrub the lemons under warm running water with a soft bristle brush to remove the wax coating. Cut into quarters, leaving the base attached at the stem end. Gently open each lemon, remove any visible pips and pack 1 tablespoon of the salt against the cut edges of each lemon. Push the lemons back into shape and pack tightly into a 2 litre (8 cup) jar with a clip or tight-fitting lid. (Depending on the size of the lemons, you may not need all 12. They should be firmly packed and fill the jar.)
2 Add 250 ml (1 cup) of the lemon juice, the peppercorns, bay leaf and remaining rock salt to the jar. Fill the jar to the top with the remaining lemon juice. Seal and shake to combine all the ingredients. Leave in a cool, dark place for 6 weeks, inverting each week. (In warm weather, store in the refrigerator.) The liquid will be cloudy initially, but will clear by the fourth week.
3 To test if the lemons are preserved, cut through the centre of one of the lemon quarters. If the pith is still

white, the lemons are not ready. Re-seal and leave for a week before testing again. The lemons should be soft-skinned and the pith should be the same colour as the skin.
4 Once the lemons are preserved, cover the brine with a layer of olive oil. Replace the oil each time you remove some of the lemon pieces.

Nutritional analysis not appropriate for this recipe.

COOK'S FILE
Storage time: Preserved lemons can be stored for up to 6 months in a cool, dark place.
Hint: Serve preserved lemons with Moroccan-flavoured dishes such as grilled (broiled) meats or use to flavour couscous, stuffings, tagines and casseroles. Only the rind is used in cooking. Discard the flesh and bitter pith, rinse and finely slice or chop the rind before adding it to the dish.

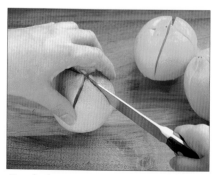

Cut the lemons into quarters, without cutting all the way through the base.

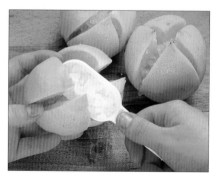

Pack the rock salt against the cut edges of each lemon.

Fill the jar to the top with the remaining lemon juice.

FOCACCIA
(Italian flatbread)

Preparation time: 30 minutes
+ 3 hours 40 minutes rising
Total cooking time: 20 minutes
Makes two loaves

½ teaspoon caster (superfine) sugar
7 g (¼ oz) sachet dry yeast
1 kg (2 lb 4 oz) bread flour (see Note)
60 ml (¼ cup) olive oil

1 Mix the sugar, dry yeast and
2 tablespoons warm water in a small
bowl. Leave in a warm place for
10 minutes, or until foamy. If it
doesn't foam the yeast is dead and
you will have to start again.
2 Place the flour in a large bowl with
2 teaspoons salt, and mix well. Add
2 tablespoons of the oil, the yeast
mixture and 750 ml (3 cups) warm
water. Mix with a wooden spoon until
it comes together in a loose dough;
turn out onto a lightly floured surface.
Start kneading to form a soft, moist,
non-sticky dough, adding a little
extra flour or warm water as needed.
Knead for 8 minutes, or until smooth.
3 Lightly oil a large bowl. Place the
dough in the bowl and roll it around.
Cut a cross on top with a sharp knife.
Cover the bowl with a tea towel and
leave in a dry, warm place for 1 hour
30 minutes, or until doubled in size.
4 Punch down the dough on a
lightly floured surface. Divide in half.
Roll one portion out to a 28 cm x
20 cm (11 inch x 8 inch) rectangle.
Use the heels of your hands to work
from the middle outwards and shape
into a 38 cm x 28 cm (15¼ inch x
11 inch) rectangle.

5 Lightly oil a baking tray and dust
with flour. Place the dough in the
centre and slide the tray inside a
plastic bag. Leave in a dry, warm place
for 2 hours, or until doubled in size.
6 Preheat the oven to 220°C (425°F/
Gas 7). Brush the dough with some
of the remaining olive oil and bake
for 20 minutes, or until golden.
Transfer to a wire rack to cool. Allow
plenty of air to circulate under the
loaf to keep the crust crisp. Repeat
with the remaining dough. Best eaten
within 6 hours of baking.

NUTRITION PER LOAF
Protein 55.5 g; Fat 35 g; Carbohydrate 368 g;
Dietary Fibre 20 g; Cholesterol 0 mg;
8468 kJ (2023 Cal)

COOK'S FILE
Note: If bread flour is unavailable, you
can use plain flour. It requires less water,
so start by adding 250 ml (1 cup) of the
water in step 2, then gradually add more
to give a soft but non-sticky dough. The
bread will have a denser texture.

*Leave the yeast mixture in a warm place
until foamy.*

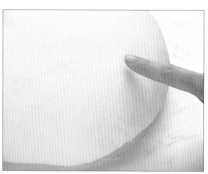

*Knead the dough until the impression
made by a finger springs out.*

*Use the heels of your hands to work from
the middle outwards.*

MARINATING OLIVES

Cracking the olives means to cut a slit around the olives using a sharp knife to allow flavours to infuse into the olives. To sterilize the storage jar, rinse with boiling water then place in a warm oven to dry. Olive oil solidifies with refrigeration, so take the olives out of the fridge 30 minutes before serving.

MIXED OLIVES WITH HERBS

Place 200 g (7 oz) small black olives (Riverina or Ligurian), 200 g (7 oz) cracked green olives, 200 g (7 oz) cracked Kalamata olives, 3 sprigs thyme, 1 tablespoon fresh oregano leaves, 1 teaspoon paprika, 2 bay leaves and 2 teaspoons lemon zest in a bowl and toss well. Spoon into a 1 litre (4 cup) sterilized wide-necked jar and add 450 ml (16 fl oz) olive oil. Marinate for 1–2 weeks in the fridge. Keeps for 1 month in the fridge.

CHILLI OLIVES

Soak 3 thinly sliced garlic cloves in vinegar or lemon juice for 24 hours. Drain and mix in a bowl with 500 g (1 lb 2 oz) cured (wrinkled) black olives, 3 tablespoons chopped fresh flat-leaf (Italian) parsley, 1 tablespoon dried chilli flakes, 3 teaspoons crushed coriander seeds and 2 teaspoons crushed cumin seeds. Spoon into a 1 litre (4 cup) sterilized wide-necked jar and add 500 ml (2 cups) olive oil. Marinate for 1–2 weeks in the fridge. Keeps for 1 month in the fridge.

ANCHOVY-STUFFED GREEN OLIVES WITH PRESERVED LEMON

Toss 500 g (1 lb 2 oz) anchovy-stuffed green olives in a bowl with 1/2 preserved lemon, pith and flesh removed, rind washed and thinly sliced, 2 tablespoons of liquid from the lemons and 1 tablespoon coriander seeds. Spoon into a 1 litre (4 cup) sterilized wide-necked jar and add 500 ml (2 cups) olive oil. Marinate for 1–2 weeks in the fridge. Will keep for 1 month in the fridge.

LEMON, THYME AND ROSEMARY OLIVES

Soak 2 thinly sliced garlic cloves in vinegar or lemon juice for 24 hours. Drain and place in a bowl with 500 g (1 lb 2 oz) cracked Kalamata olives, 2 crushed bay leaves, 4 slices lemon, cut into quarters, 3 sprigs fresh thyme, 1 sprig of fresh rosemary, 1/2 teaspoon black peppercorns and 60 ml (1/4 cup) lemon juice, and toss to combine. Spoon into a 1 litre (4 cup) sterilized wide-necked jar and pour in 500 ml (2 cups) olive oil. Marinate for 1–2 weeks in the fridge. Will keep for 1 month in the fridge.

CORIANDER AND ORANGE OLIVES

Place 500 g (1 lb 2 oz) jumbo green olives in a large bowl and add 2 teaspoons crushed coriander seeds, 3 teaspoons orange zest, 60 ml (1/4 cup) orange juice, 1/4 teaspoon cayenne pepper, 3 tablespoons chopped fresh coriander (cilantro) leaves and toss to combine thoroughly. Carefully spoon into a 1 litre (4 cup), sterilized wide-necked jar and pour in 500 ml (2 cups) olive oil or enough to completely cover. Leave to marinate for 1–2 weeks in the fridge. Will keep for 1 month in the fridge.

FENNEL, ORANGE AND DILL OLIVES

Soak 2 thinly sliced garlic cloves in vinegar or lemon juice for 24 hours. Drain and place the garlic in a large bowl with 500 g (1 lb 2 oz) cracked black olives, 4 thin slices orange, cut into quarters, 2 teaspoons crushed fennel seeds and 2 tablespoons chopped fresh dill and toss to combine well. Spoon into a 1 litre (4 cup) sterilized wide necked jar and pour in 500 ml (2 cups) olive oil or enough to completely cover. Marinate for 1–2 weeks in the fridge. Will keep for 1 month in the fridge.

Left to right: Mixed olives with herbs; Chilli olives; Anchovy-stuffed green olives with preserved lemon; Lemon, thyme and rosemary olives; Coriander and orange olives; Fennel, orange and dill olives.

BUNUELOS DE BACALAO
(Salt cod fritters)

Preparation time: 15 minutes
  + 24 hours soaking
Total cooking time: 50 minutes
Makes 35

500 g (1 lb 2 oz) salt cod
1 large potato (200 g/7 oz), unpeeled
2 tablespoons milk
olive oil, for deep-frying
1 small onion, finely chopped
2 garlic cloves, crushed
30 g (¼ cup) self-raising flour
2 eggs, separated
1 tablespoon finely chopped fresh
   flat-leaf (Italian) parsley

1 Soak the cod in water for 24 hours, changing the water regularly. Bring a saucepan of water to the boil, add the potato and cook for 20 minutes, or until soft. When cool enough to handle, peel and mash with the milk and 2 tablespoons of the olive oil.
2 Drain the cod, cut into large pieces and place in a saucepan. Cover with water, bring to the boil over high heat, then reduce the heat to medium and cook for 10 minutes, or until soft and a froth forms on the surface. Drain. When cool enough to handle, remove the skin and any bones, then mash with a fork until flaky. (You should have about 200 g/7 oz).
3 Meanwhile, heat 1 tablespoon olive oil in a frying pan, add the onion and cook over medium heat for 5 minutes,

or until softened and starting to brown. Add the garlic and cook for 1 minute. Remove from the heat.
4 Combine the potato, cod, onion mixture, flour, egg yolks and parsley in a bowl and season. Whisk the egg whites until stiff then fold into the mixture. Fill a large heavy-based saucepan one third full with olive oil and heat to 190°C (375°F), or until a cube of bread dropped in the oil browns in 10 seconds. Drop heaped tablespoons of the mixture into the oil and cook for 2 minutes, or until puffed and golden. Drain on paper towels and serve immediately.

NUTRITION PER FRITTER
Protein 3 g; Fat 3 g; Carbohydrate 1.5 g; Dietary Fibre 0 g; Cholesterol 17 mg; 198 kJ (47 Cal)

Remove the skin and any bones from the cooked salt cod.

Fold the whisked egg whites into the potato and cod mixture.

Deep-fry the fritters in hot oil until puffed and golden.

STUFFED SARDINES

Preparation time: 30 minutes
Total cooking time: 30 minutes
Serves 6

750 g (1 lb 10 oz) small fresh sardines
2 teaspoons olive oil
100 g (3½ oz) ling fillet or other white
 firm-fleshed fish
600 g (1 lb 5 oz) cooked medium
 prawns (shrimp), peeled, deveined
45 g (¼ cup) cooked arborio or other
 medium-grain rice
3 garlic cloves, crushed
1 tablespoon finely chopped fresh
 mint
1 tablespoon finely chopped fresh
 basil
1 tablespoon finely chopped fresh
 chives
2 tablespoons grated Parmesan
 cheese
2 teaspoons lemon juice
1 egg, lightly beaten
3 tablespoons fresh breadcrumbs
2 tablespoons olive oil
olive oil, extra, to serve
lemon juice, extra, to serve

1 Preheat the oven to 180°C (350°F/ Gas 4). Grease a shallow 30 cm x 25 cm (12 inch x 10 inch) ovenproof dish.
2 Remove the heads, tails and fins from the sardines. Make a slit along the underside, and remove the intestines and backbone. Rinse and pat dry. Trim the edges of 24 sardines and lay them out flat on a work surface, skin-side-down. Finely chop the remainder and place in a bowl.
3 Heat the oil in a frying pan and cook the ling over medium heat for 4–5 minutes each side, or until

cooked. Do not overbrown. Flake and add to the chopped sardines. Finely chop the prawns and add to the bowl along with the rice, garlic, mint, basil, chives, Parmesan and lemon juice. Mix, then season and stir in the egg.
4 Place 12 butterflied sardines in the prepared dish, skin-side-down and side-by-side. Divide the filling among them, covering each fillet and pressing firmly onto it. Cover with the remaining sardines, skin-side-up. Scatter the breadcrumbs over the top and drizzle with the olive oil. Bake for 20–25 minutes, or until golden.

Drizzle with oil and lemon juice and serve.

NUTRITION PER SERVE
Protein 27 g; Fat 11 g; Carbohydrate 8.5 g; Dietary Fibre 0 g; Cholesterol 194 mg; 1023 kJ (244 Cal)

COOK'S FILE
Note: If only large sardines are available, trim those butterflied to 8 cm x 4 cm (3 inch x 1½ inch) and use 120 g (4 oz) chopped for the filling. If buying butterflied sardines, you will need 400 g (14 oz). Cod is traditional for this recipe, but ling or any firm, white fish works well.

Make a slit along the underside of the sardines with a very sharp knife.

Remove the intestines and then the backbones, and rinse under cold water.

Place the remaining sardines over the mixture, skin-side-up.

MELITZANOSALATA
(Greek puréed roasted eggplant salad)

Preparation time: 20 minutes
  + 3 hours refrigeration
Total cooking time: 1 hour
Serves 6

2 large eggplants (aubergines)
2 garlic cloves, roughly chopped
4 tablespoons chopped fresh flat-leaf
  (Italian) parsley
1 small onion, grated
1/2 red capsicum (pepper), seeded and
  chopped

1 large ripe tomato, finely chopped
2 small red chillies, seeded
60 g (3/4 cup) soft white breadcrumbs
80 ml (1/3 cup) lemon juice
125 ml (1/2 cup) good-quality olive oil
1–2 tablespoons olive oil, extra
7 black olives

1 Preheat the oven to 180°C (350°F/ Gas 4). Prick the eggplants with a fork a few times, place on a large baking tray and bake for 1 hour.
2 Remove the skin from the eggplant and discard. Roughly chop the flesh and place in a sieve to drain. Press the flesh against the sieve with the back of a knife.
3 Place the eggplant, garlic, parsley,

onion, capsicum, tomato, chilli and breadcrumbs in a food processor, season and process until combined but a little coarse.
4 While the motor is running, add the lemon juice and oil alternately, in a steady stream. The mixture will thicken.
5 Transfer to a large bowl, cover and refrigerate for 3 hours to firm the mixture and infuse the flavours. To serve, spread on a large shallow serving platter, drizzle with the extra oil and garnish with black olives.

NUTRITION PER SERVE
Protein 3.8 g; Fat 2.7 g; Carbohydrate 12.5 g; Dietary Fibre 5 g; Cholesterol 0 mg; 383 kJ (92 Cal)

Wear gloves when handling chillies to protect your hands.

Remove the skin from the eggplant and roughly chop the flesh.

Process the ingredients until they are combined, but still a little coarse.

DOLMADES
(Greek vine leaf parcels)

Preparation time: 40 minutes
  + 15 minutes soaking
Total cooking time: 45 minutes
Makes 24

200 g (7 oz) packet vine leaves in
  brine
250 g (1 cup) medium-grain rice
1 small onion, finely chopped
1 tablespoon olive oil
50 g (1³/4 oz) pine nuts, toasted
2 tablespoons currants
2 tablespoons chopped fresh dill
1 tablespoon finely chopped fresh mint
1 tablespoon finely chopped fresh
  flat-leaf (Italian) parsley
80 ml (¹/3 cup) olive oil, extra
2 tablespoons lemon juice
500 ml (2 cups) chicken stock or
  vegetable stock

1 Place the vine leaves in a bowl, cover with hot water and soak for 15 minutes. Remove and pat dry. Cut off any stems. Reserve some leaves to line the saucepan and discard any that have holes. Meanwhile, soak the rice in boiling water for 10 minutes to soften, then drain.
2 Place the rice, onion, oil, pine nuts, currants, herbs and salt and pepper in a large bowl, and mix well.
3 Lay some leaves vein-side-down on a flat surface. Place 1 tablespoon of filling in the middle of each leaf, fold the stalk end over the filling, then the left and right sides into the middle, and finally roll firmly towards the tip. The dolmade should resemble a small cigar. Repeat with the remaining filling and leaves.

4 Using the reserved vine leaves, line the bottom of a large heavy-based pan. Drizzle with 1 tablespoon of the extra oil. Place the dolmades in the pan, packing tightly in one layer. Pour the remaining lemon juice and oil on top.
5 Pour the stock over the dolmades and cover with an inverted plate to stop them moving around while cooking. Bring to the boil, then reduce the heat and simmer, covered,

for 45 minutes. Remove with a slotted spoon. Serve warm or cold.

NUTRITION PER DOLMADE
Protein 1 g; Fat 5.5 g; Carbohydrate 8.5 g;
Dietary Fibre 0 g; Cholesterol 0 mg;
370 kJ (89 Cal)

COOK'S FILE
Note: Any unused leaves can be stored in brine in an airtight container in the refrigerator for up to 1 week.

Fold the sides of the vine leaf into the middle and roll up towards the tip.

Pack the dolmades tightly into the pan and pour on the oil and lemon juice.

Remove the cooked dolmades from the pan with a slotted spoon.

FRITTO MISTO DI MARE
(Fried seafood salad)

Preparation time: 20 minutes
Total cooking time: 10 minutes
Serves 4

200 g (7 oz) cuttlefish
800 g (1 lb 12 oz) red mullet fillets
1/2 teaspoon paprika
75 g (2 1/2 oz) plain (all-purpose) flour
12 raw medium prawns (shrimp),
    peeled, deveined, tails intact
good-quality olive oil, for deep-frying
lemon wedges, to serve

1 Preheat the oven to 150°C (300°F/ Gas 2). Line a large baking tray with baking paper. Place the cuttlefish bone-side-down on a board and, using a sharp knife, gently cut lengthways through the body. Open out, remove the cuttlebone and then gently remove the insides. Cut the flesh in half. Under cold running water, pull the skin away. Cut the cuttlefish and mullet into even-size pieces. Pat dry well with paper towels. Season with salt and freshly ground black pepper. Mix the paprika and flour together in a bowl, add the seafood and toss to coat. Shake off any excess flour.

2 Fill a deep heavy-based saucepan one third full of oil and heat to 190°C (375°F), or until a cube of bread dropped in the oil browns in 10 seconds. Add the seafood in batches and cook for 1 minute, or until golden and cooked through. Drain on crumpled paper towels. Keep warm on the baking tray in the oven while you cook the rest.
3 Place all the seafood on a serving platter. Sprinkle with extra salt and serve with lemon wedges.

NUTRITION PER SERVE
Protein 40 g; Fat 14 g; Carbohydrate 14 g; Dietary Fibre 0 g; Cholesterol 176 mg; 1433 kJ (342 Cal)

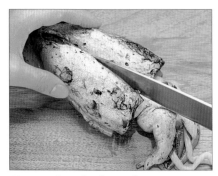

Using a sharp knife, gently cut lengthways through the cuttlefish body.

Remove the cuttlebone and the insides from the cuttlefish.

Add the seafood to the flour and paprika mixture and toss to coat.

LENTIL AND BURGHUL FRITTERS WITH YOGHURT SAUCE

Preparation time: 20 minutes
    + 1 hour 30 minutes standing
Total cooking time:
    1 hour 10 minutes
Makes 35

140 g (³/4 cup) brown lentils, rinsed
90 g (¹/2 cup) burghul
80 ml (¹/3 cup) olive oil
1 onion, finely chopped
2 garlic cloves, finely chopped
3 teaspoons ground cumin
2 teaspoons ground coriander
3 tablespoons finely chopped fresh
    mint leaves
4 eggs, lightly beaten
60 g (¹/2 cup) plain (all-purpose) flour
1 teaspoon sea salt

Yoghurt sauce
1 small Lebanese (short) cucumber,
    peeled
250 g (1 cup) Greek-style plain yoghurt
1–2 garlic cloves, finely chopped

1 Place the lentils in a saucepan with 625 ml (2¹/2 cups) water. Bring to the boil, then reduce the heat and simmer for 30 minutes, or until tender.
2 Remove from the heat and add water to just cover the lentils. Pour in the burghul, cover and stand for 1¹/2 hours, or until the burghul has expanded. Transfer to a bowl.
3 To make the yoghurt sauce, halve the cucumber, scoop out the seeds and discard. Grate the flesh and place in a bowl with the yoghurt and garlic, and mix together well.
4 Heat half the oil in a frying pan over medium heat. Cook the onion and garlic for 5 minutes, or until soft. Add the cumin and coriander.
5 Add the onion mixture, mint, eggs, flour and sea salt to the lentil mixture, and mix together well. The mixture should be thick enough to drop spoonfuls into the pan. If the mixture is too wet, add a little extra flour.
6 Heat the remaining oil in the cleaned frying pan over medium heat. Working in batches, drop heaped tablespoons of mixture into the pan. Cook for 3 minutes each side, or until browned. Drain, season with salt and serve with the yoghurt sauce.

NUTRITION PER FRITTER
Protein 2.5 g; Fat 3 g; Carbohydrate 5 g; Dietary Fibre 1 g; Cholesterol 22 mg; 245 kJ (60 Cal)

Add the burghul to the lentils and leave to stand for 1 hour 30 minutes.

Combine the lentil mixture, onion mixture, mint, eggs, flour and sea salt.

Cook the fritters in a frying pan until browned on both sides.

VEGETABLE DISHES

PIZZA MARGHERITA
(Italian tomato, bocconcini and basil pizza)

Preparation time: 25 minutes
   + 1 hour rising
Total cooking time: 45 minutes
Serves 6–8

225 g (8 oz) white bread flour
1 teaspoon sugar
7 g (1/4 oz) sachet dry yeast
2 tablespoons olive oil
90 ml (3 fl oz) milk
1 garlic clove, crushed
425 g (15 oz) can crushed tomatoes
1 bay leaf
1 teaspoon chopped fresh thyme
6 fresh basil leaves, chopped
150 g (51/2 oz) bocconcini, thinly sliced
olive oil, extra, to drizzle

1 Place the flour, sugar, yeast and
1/2 teaspoon salt in a large bowl.
Combine half the olive oil with the
milk and 80 ml (1/3 cup) warm
water—add to the dry ingredients. Stir
with a wooden spoon to combine.
2 Place on a lightly floured work
surface and knead for 5 minutes, or
until soft and smooth. Lightly oil a
bowl, add the dough and turn to coat
in the oil. Leave in a warm place for
1 hour, or until doubled in size.
Preheat the oven to 210°C (415°F/
Gas 6–7).
3 Meanwhile, heat the remaining oil
in a saucepan over medium heat, add
the garlic and cook, stirring, for
30 seconds. Add the tomato, bay leaf,
thyme and basil and simmer, stirring
occasionally, for 20–25 minutes, or
until thick and fragrant. Allow to
cool. Remove the bay leaf.
4 Place the dough on a lightly floured
work surface, then punch down to
expel the air and knead for 5 minutes.
Shape the dough into a neat ball and
roll out to a 28–30 cm (11–12 inch)
diameter. Lightly oil a 28–30 cm
(11–12 inch) pizza tray and place the
dough on the tray. Spread the tomato
sauce over the dough, leaving a 3 cm
(11/4 inch) border. Arrange the
bocconcini over the sauce, drizzle
with olive oil and bake for 15 minutes,
or until crisp and bubbling.

NUTRITION PER SERVE (8)
Protein 8 g; Fat 9 g; Carbohydrate 24 g;
Dietary Fibre 2 g; Cholesterol 11 mg;
870 kJ (207 Cal)

COOK'S FILE
Note: The red, white and green
toppings of this pizza symbolize the
Italian flag.

*Roll the pizza dough out to a 28 cm–30 cm
(11inch x 12 inch) diameter.*

*Arrange the bocconcini slices over the
tomato sauce.*

41

FATTOUSH
(Lebanese toasted bread salad)

Preparation time: 15 minutes
Total cooking time: 10 minutes
Serves 6

2 pitta bread rounds (17 cm/7 inch)
6 cos (romaine) lettuce leaves, shredded
1 large Lebanese (short) cucumber, cubed
4 tomatoes, cut into 1 cm (1/2 inch) cubes
8 spring onions (scallions), chopped

4 tablespoons finely chopped fresh flat-leaf (Italian) parsley
1 tablespoon finely chopped fresh mint
2 tablespoons finely chopped fresh coriander (cilantro)

Dressing
2 garlic cloves, crushed
100 ml (3 1/2 fl oz) extra virgin olive oil
100 ml (3 1/2 fl oz) lemon juice

1 Preheat the oven to 180°C (350°F/Gas 4). Split the bread in half through the centre and bake on a baking tray for 8–10 minutes, or until golden and crisp, turning halfway

through. Break into pieces.
2 To make the dressing, whisk all the ingredients together until combined.
3 Place the bread and remaining salad ingredients in a serving bowl and toss to combine. Pour on the dressing and toss well. Season. Serve immediately.

NUTRITION PER SERVE
Protein 5.5 g; Fat 17 g; Carbohydrate 24 g; Dietary Fibre 4 g; Cholesterol 0 mg; 1133 kJ (270 Cal)

COOK'S FILE
Note: This is a popular Middle Eastern peasant salad which is served as an appetizer or to accompany a light meal.

Split the pitta bread rounds in two through the centre.

Once the bread is golden and crisp, break it into small pieces.

Place the bread pieces and salad ingredients in a bowl and toss well.

ROASTED FENNEL AND ORANGE SALAD

Preparation time: 30 minutes
Total cooking time: 1 hour
Serves 4

8 baby fennel bulbs
100 ml (3½ fl oz) olive oil
1 teaspoon sea salt
2 oranges
1 tablespoon lemon juice
1 red onion, halved and thinly sliced
100 g (3½ oz) Kalamata olives
2 tablespoons chopped fresh mint
1 tablespoon roughly chopped fresh
    flat-leaf (Italian) parsley

1 Preheat the oven to 200°C (400°F/ Gas 6). Trim and reserve the fennel fronds. Remove the stalks and cut a 5 mm (¼ inch) slice off the base of each fennel bilb. Slice each fennel into 6 wedges. Place in a baking dish and drizzle with 60 ml (¼ cup) of the oil. Add the salt and plenty of pepper. Bake for 40–60 minutes, or until the fennel is tender and slightly caramelized. Cool.

2 Cut a slice off the top and bottom of each orange. Using a small sharp knife, slice off the skin and pith, following the curves of the orange. Remove as much pith as possible. Slice down the side of a segment between the flesh and the membrane. Repeat with the other side and lift the segment out. Do this over a bowl to catch the segments and juices. Repeat with all the segments. Squeeze any juice from the membrane. Drain and reserve the juice.

3 Whisk the remaining olive oil into the orange juice and the lemon juice until emulsified. Season well. Combine the orange segments, onion and olives in a bowl, pour on half the dressing and add half the mint. Mix well. Transfer to a serving dish. Top with the roasted fennel, drizzle with the remaining dressing, and scatter with the parsley and the remaining mint. Roughly chop the reserved fronds and scatter over the salad.

NUTRITION PER SERVE
Protein 5 g; Fat 25 g; Carbohydrate 19 g; Dietary Fibre 15 g; Cholesterol 0 mg; 1339 kJ (320 Cal)

Use a sharp knife to slice each of the baby fennels into wedges.

Bake the fennel until tender and slightly caramelized.

Remove the orange skin and pith with a small sharp knife.

Cut the orange between the flesh and the membrane to remove the segments.

WARM CHICKPEA AND SILVERBEET SALAD WITH SUMAC

Preparation time: 30 minutes
  + overnight soaking
Total cooking time: 2 hours
Serves 4

250 g (9 oz) dried chickpeas
125 ml (1/2 cup) olive oil
1 onion, cut into thin wedges
2 tomatoes
1 teaspoon sugar
1/4 teaspoon ground cinnamon
2 garlic cloves, chopped

1.5 kg (3 lb 5 oz) silverbeet (Swiss chard)
3 tablespoons chopped fresh mint
2–3 tablespoons lemon juice
1 1/2 tablespoons ground sumac (see Note)

1 Place the chickpeas in a large bowl, cover with water and leave to soak overnight. Drain and place in a large saucepan. Cover with water and bring to the boil, then simmer for 1 3/4 hours, or until tender. Drain.
2 Heat the oil in a frying pan, add the onion and cook over low heat for 3–4 minutes, or until soft and just starting to brown. Cut the tomatoes in half, remove the seeds and dice the

flesh. Add to the pan with the sugar, cinnamon and garlic, and cook for 2–3 minutes, or until softened.
3 Wash the silverbeet and dry with paper towel. Trim the stems and shred the leaves. Add to the tomato mix with the chickpeas; cook for 3–4 minutes, or until the silverbeet wilts. Add the mint, lemon juice and sumac; season, and cook for 1 minute. Serve at once.

NUTRITION PER SERVE
Protein 18 g; Fat 34 g; Carbohydrate 30 g; Dietary Fibre 20 g; Cholesterol 0 mg; 2080 kJ (497 Cal)

COOK'S FILE
Note: Sumac is available from Middle Eastern speciality shops.

Scoop the seeds out of the halved tomatoes with a teaspoon.

Add the tomato, sugar, cinnamon and garlic to the pan and cook until soft.

Add the silverbeet and chickpeas and cook until the spinach is wilted.

HORIATIKI SALATA
(Greek salad)

Preparation time: 20 minutes
Total cooking time: Nil
Serves 4

4 tomatoes, cut into wedges
1 telegraph cucumber, peeled, halved, seeded and cut into small cubes
2 green capsicums (peppers), seeded, halved lengthways and cut into strips
1 red onion, finely sliced
16 Kalamata olives
250 g (9 oz) good-quality firm feta, cut into cubes
3 tablespoons fresh flat-leaf (Italian) parsley leaves
12 whole fresh mint leaves
125 ml (½ cup) good-quality olive oil
2 tablespoons lemon juice
1 garlic clove, crushed

1 Place the tomato, cucumber, capsicum, onion, olives, feta and half the parsley and mint leaves in a large salad bowl, and gently mix together.
2 Place the oil, lemon juice and garlic in a screw-top jar, season and shake until combined. Pour over the salad and lightly toss. Garnish with the remaining parsley and mint.

NUTRITION PER SERVE
Protein 15 g; Fat 45 g; Carbohydrate 7.5 g; Dietary Fibre 4 g; Cholesterol 43 mg; 2015 kJ (493 Cal)

Peel, halve and seed the cucumber, then cut into small cubes.

Cut the good-quality firm feta into even-sized cubes.

Gently mix the salad ingredients together, without breaking up the feta.

SALATET ADS
(Lentil salad)

Preparation time: 15 minutes
  + 30 minutes standing
Total cooking time: 30 minutes
Serves 4–6

1/2 brown onion
2 cloves
300 g (1 1/2 cups) puy lentils (see Note)
1 strip lemon rind
2 garlic cloves, peeled
1 fresh bay leaf

2 teaspoons ground cumin
2 tablespoons red wine vinegar
60 ml (1/4 cup) olive oil
1 tablespoon lemon juice
2 tablespoon fresh mint leaves,
  finely chopped
3 spring onions (scallions), finely
  chopped

1 Stud the onion with the cloves and place in a saucepan with the lentils, rind, garlic, bay leaf, 1 teaspoon cumin and 875 ml (3 1/2 cups) water. Bring to the boil and cook over medium heat for 25–30 minutes, or until the water absorbs. Discard the onion, rind and bay leaf. Reserve the garlic; finely chop.
2 Whisk together the vinegar, oil, juice, garlic and remaining cumin. Stir through the lentils with the mint and spring onion. Season well. Leave for 30 minutes to let the flavours absorb. Serve at room temperature.

NUTRITION PER SERVE (6)
Protein 13 g; Fat 11 g; Carbohydrate 20 g;
Dietary Fibre 7.5 g; Cholesterol 0 mg;
930 kJ (222 Cal)

COOK'S FILE
Note: Puy lentils are small, green lentils from France. They are available dried from gourmet food stores.

Stud the brown onion half with the cloves.

Cook the lentils, then discard the onion, lemon rind and bay leaf.

Whisk together the vinegar, oil, lemon juice, garlic and cumin.

PARMIGIANA DI MELANZANE
(Italian baked eggplant with tomato and mozzarella)

Preparation time: 20 minutes
Total cooking time: 40 minutes
Serves 6

6 large slender eggplants (aubergines) (700 g/1 lb 9 oz)
80 ml (⅓ cup) olive oil
1 tablespoon olive oil, extra
2 onions, finely chopped
2 garlic cloves, crushed
400 g (14 oz) can diced tomatoes
1 tablespoon tomato paste (purée)
3 tablespoons chopped fresh flat-leaf (Italian) parsley
1 tablespoon chopped fresh oregano
1 teaspoon sugar
125 g (4½ oz) mozzarella, grated

1 Preheat the oven to 180°C (350°F/ Gas 4). Cut the eggplants in half lengthways, keeping the stems attached. Score the flesh by cutting a criss-cross pattern with a sharp knife, being careful not to cut through the skin. Heat half the oil in a large frying pan, add half the eggplant and cook for 2–3 minutes each side, or until the flesh is soft. Remove. Repeat with the remaining oil and eggplant. Cool slightly. Scoop out the flesh, leaving a 2 mm (⅛ inch) border. Finely chop the flesh and reserve the shells.
2 In the same pan, heat the extra oil and cook the onion over medium heat for 5 minutes. Add the garlic and cook for 30 seconds, then add the tomato, tomato paste, herbs, sugar and eggplant flesh, and cook, stirring occasionally, over low heat for 8–10 minutes, or until the sauce is thick and pulpy. Season.
3 Arrange the eggplant shells in a lightly greased baking dish and spoon in the tomato filling. Sprinkle with the mozzarella and bake for 5–10 minutes, or until the cheese has melted.

NUTRITION PER SERVE
Protein 7.5 g; Fat 20 g; Carbohydrate 6 g; Dietary Fibre 3.5 g; Cholesterol 13 mg; 997 kJ (238 Cal)

Score the eggplant in a criss-cross pattern without cutting the skin.

Scoop the flesh out of the cooked eggplant, leaving a narrow border.

Spoon the tomato filling into the eggplant shells.

POLENTA SQUARES WITH MUSHROOM RAGU

Preparation time: 25 minutes
 + 20 minutes refrigeration
 + 10 minutes standing
Total cooking time: 40 minutes
Serves 4

500 ml (2 cups) vegetable stock
150 g (1 cup) medium-grain polenta
20 g (1/2 oz) butter
75 g (3/4 cup) grated Parmesan
 cheese
5 g (1/8 oz) dried porcini mushrooms
200 g (7 oz) Swiss brown mushrooms
300 g (10 1/2 oz) field mushrooms
125 ml (1/2 cup) olive oil
1 onion, chopped
3 garlic cloves, finely chopped
1 fresh bay leaf
2 teaspoons chopped fresh thyme
2 teaspoons chopped fresh oregano
15 g (1/2 cup) finely chopped fresh
 flat-leaf (Italian) parsley
1 tablespoon balsamic vinegar
25 g (1/4 cup) grated Parmesan
 cheese, extra

1 Place the stock and a pinch of salt in a large saucepan and bring to the boil. Add the polenta in a steady stream, stirring constantly. Reduce the heat and simmer, stirring occasionally, for 15–20 minutes. Remove from the heat and stir in the butter and Parmesan.
2 Grease a 20 cm (8 inch) square shallow cake tin, spread the mixture into the tin. Refrigerate for 20 minutes.
3 Soak the porcini mushrooms in 125 ml (1/2 cup) boiling water for 10 minutes, or until softened. Drain, reserving 80 ml (1/3 cup) liquid. Wipe the mushrooms with a damp cloth to remove any dirt. Thickly slice the Swiss brown mushrooms, and coarsely chop the field mushrooms. Heat 80 ml (1/3 cup) olive oil in a large frying pan, add the mushrooms and cook for 4–5 minutes. Remove from the pan. Heat the remaining oil in the pan, add the onion and cook over medium heat for 2–3 minutes, or until transparent.
4 Add the reserved soaking liquid, garlic, bay leaf, thyme and oregano, season and cook for 1 minute. Return the mushrooms to the pan and add the parsley and balsamic vinegar, and cook over medium heat for 1 minute. Remove the bay leaf.
5 Sprinkle the extra Parmesan over the polenta. Place under a medium grill (broiler) for 10 minutes, or until lightly brown and the cheese melts. Cut into four 10 cm (4 inch) squares.
6 Place a polenta square in the centre of each serving plate and top with the mushrooms. Season with pepper.

NUTRITION PER SERVE
Protein 16 g; Fat 43 g; Carbohydrate 30 g; Dietary Fibre 3.5 g; Cholesterol 37 mg; 2354 kJ (562 Cal)

Spread the polenta mixture into the prepared cake tin.

Add the chopped parsley and balsamic vinegar to the mushroom mixture.

Sprinkle Parmesan over the polenta and grill (broil) until the cheese has melted.

PUMPKIN RISOTTO

Preparation time: 25 minutes
Total cooking time: 1 hour
Serves 4–6

600 g (1 lb 5 oz) pumpkin, cut into
   1 cm (1/2 inch) cubes
3 tablespoons olive oil
500 ml (2 cups) vegetable stock
1 onion, finely chopped
2 garlic cloves, finely chopped
1 tablespoon chopped fresh rosemary
440 g (2 cups) arborio rice
125 ml (1/2 cup) white wine
30 g (1 oz) butter
35 g (1/3 cup) grated Parmesan
   cheese
3 tablespoons finely chopped fresh
   flat-leaf (Italian) parsley

1 Preheat the oven to 200°C (400°F/ Gas 6). Toss the pieces of pumpkin in 2 tablespoons of the oil, place in a baking dish and roast for 30 minutes, or until tender and golden. Turn the pumpkin pieces halfway through the cooking time.

2 Heat the stock and 750 ml (3 cups) water in a saucepan, cover and keep at a low simmer.

3 Heat the remaining oil in a large saucepan, and cook the onion, garlic and rosemary, stirring, over low heat for 5 minutes, or until the onion is cooked but not browned. Add the rice and stir to coat. Stir in the wine for 2–3 minutes, or until absorbed.

4 Add 125 ml (1/2 cup) stock, stirring constantly over medium heat until all the liquid is absorbed. Continue adding stock 125 ml (1/2 cup) at a time, stirring constantly for 20 minutes, or until all the stock is absorbed and the rice is tender and creamy. Season to taste with salt and freshly ground black pepper and stir in the pumpkin, butter, Parmesan and parsley. Serve immediately.

NUTRITION PER SERVE (6)
Protein 6 g; Fat 16 g; Carbohydrate 20 g; Dietary Fibre 2 g; Cholesterol 18 mg; 1052 kJ (250 Cal)

Add the wine to the rice and stir until absorbed.

Gradually add the stock to the rice until it is all absorbed and the rice is tender.

Stir the pumpkin, butter, Parmesan and parsley through the rice.

RATATOUILLE
(French vegetable stew)

Preparation time: 30 minutes
Total cooking time: 40 minutes
Serves 4–6

6 vine-ripened tomatoes
5 tablespoons olive oil
500 g (1 lb 2 oz) eggplant (aubergine),
    cut into 2 cm (¾ inch) cubes
375 g (13 oz) zucchini (courgette), cut
    into 2 cm (¾ inch) slices
1 green capsicum (pepper), seeded,
    cut into 2 cm (¾ inch) cubes
1 red onion, cut into wedges
3 garlic cloves, finely chopped
2 teaspoons chopped fresh thyme
¼ teaspoon cayenne pepper
2 bay leaves
1 tablespoon red wine vinegar
1 teaspoon caster (superfine) sugar
3 tablespoons shredded fresh basil

1 Score a cross in the base of each tomato. Place in a bowl of boiling water for 1 minute, then plunge into cold water and peel the skin away from the cross. Roughly chop.
2 Heat 2 tablespoons oil in a large saucepan and cook the eggplant over medium heat for 4–5 minutes, or until soft but not browned. Remove. Add 2 tablespoons oil to the pan and cook the zucchini for 3–4 minutes, or until softened. Remove from the pan. Add the capsicum to the pan, cook for 2 minutes, then remove.
3 Heat the remaining oil, add the onion and cook for 2–3 minutes, or until softened. Add the garlic, thyme, cayenne and bay leaves. Cook, stirring, for 1 minute. Return the vegetables to the pan. Add the tomato, vinegar and sugar. Simmer for 20 minutes, stirring occasionally. Stir in the basil. Season. Serve hot or cold.

NUTRITION PER SERVE (6)
Protein 4 g; Fat 17 g; Carbohydrate 8.5 g;
Dietary Fibre 5.5 g; Cholesterol 0 mg;
826 kJ (197 Cal)

COOK'S FILE
Note: Ratatouille takes quite a long time to prepare and so is traditionally made in large quantities. It is then eaten over several days as an hors d'oeuvre, side dish or main meal.

Peel the skin away from the cross cut in the base of the tomato.

Cook the eggplant until softened but not browned, then remove.

Simmer the mixture for 20 minutes, stirring occasionally.

INSALATA CAPRESE
(Tomato and bocconcini salad)

Preparation time: 10 minutes
Total cooking time: Nil
Serves 4

3 large vine-ripened tomatoes
250 g (9 oz) bocconcini (see Note)
12 fresh basil leaves
60 ml (¼ cup) extra virgin olive oil
4 basil leaves, roughly torn, extra, optional

1 Slice the tomatoes into 1 cm (½ inch) slices, making twelve slices altogether. Slice the bocconcini into twenty-four 1 cm (½ inch) slices.
2 Arrange the tomato slices on a serving plate, alternating them with 2 slices of bocconcini. Place the basil leaves between the bocconcini slices.
3 Drizzle with the oil, sprinkle with the basil, if desired, and season well with salt and ground black pepper.

NUTRITION PER SERVE
Protein 14 g; Fat 25 g; Carbohydrate 3 g; Dietary Fibre 1 g; Cholesterol 33 mg; 1221 kJ (292 Cal)

COOK'S FILE
Note: This popular summer salad is most successful with very fresh buffalo mozzarella if you can find it. We've used bocconcini in this recipe as it can be difficult to find very fresh mozzarella.

Slice the bocconcini into twenty-four 1 cm (½ inch) thick slices.

Arrange the tomato slices on a serving plate, alternating with the bocconcini.

SPANOKOPITA
(Greek spinach and cheese filo pie)

Preparation time: 25 minutes
+ cooling
Total cooking time: 1 hour
Serves 4–6

1.5 kg (3 lb 5 oz) silverbeet (Swiss chard)
3 tablespoons olive oil
1 white onion, finely chopped
10 spring onions (scallions), chopped (include some green)
1½ tablespoons chopped fresh dill
200 g (7 oz) Greek feta, crumbled
125 g (4½ oz) cottage cheese
3 tablespoons finely grated kefalotyri cheese (see Note)
¼ teaspoon ground nutmeg
4 eggs, lightly beaten
10 sheets filo pastry
80 g (2¾ oz) butter, melted, for brushing

1 Rinse and drain the silverbeet thoroughly. Discard the stems and shred the leaves. Heat the olive oil in a large frying pan, add the onion and cook, stirring, over medium heat for 5 minutes, or until softened. Add the spring onion and silverbeet and cook, covered, over medium heat for 5 minutes. Add the dill and cook, uncovered, for 3–4 minutes, or until most of the liquid has evaporated. Remove from the heat and cool to room temperature.
2 Preheat the oven to 180°C (350°F/ Gas 4) and grease a 20 cm x 25 cm (8 inch x 10 inch) 2.5 litre (10 cup) baking dish. Place the cheeses in a bowl, stir in the silverbeet mixture; add the nutmeg. Gradually add the egg; beat after each addition. Season.
3 Line the base and sides of the baking dish with a sheet of filo pastry. Brush with butter and cover with another sheet. Repeat using five sheets. Spoon in the filling and level the surface. Fold any exposed pastry up and over to cover the filling. Cover with a sheet of filo, brush with butter and continue until all the sheets are used. Roughly trim the pastry with kitchen scissors then tuck the excess inside the wall of the dish.

4 Brush the top with butter. Using a sharp knife, score the surface into diamonds. Sprinkle a few drops of cold water on top to discourage the pastry from curling. Bake for 45 minutes, or until the pastry is puffed and golden. Leave to rest at room temperature for 10 minutes before serving.

Spoon the spinach and cheese mixture into the filo-lined dish.

NUTRITION PER SERVE (6)
Protein 21 g; Fat 36 g; Carbohydrate 15 g; Dietary Fibre 8 g; Cholesterol 189 mg; 1940 kJ (463 Cal)

COOK'S FILE
Note: Use pecorino cheese if kefalotyri is unavailable.

Cover with the remaining filo pastry sheets, then tuck in the excess pastry.

LUBYI BI ZAYT
(Green beans with tomato and olive oil)

Preparation time: 10 minutes
Total cooking time: 25 minutes
Serves 4

80 ml (1/3 cup) olive oil
1 large onion, chopped
3 garlic cloves, finely chopped

400 g (14 oz) can diced tomatoes
1/2 teaspoon sugar
750 g (1 lb 10 oz) green beans, trimmed
3 tablespoons chopped fresh flat-leaf (Italian) parsley

1 Heat the olive oil in a large frying pan, add the onion and cook over medium heat for 4–5 minutes, or until softened. Add the garlic and cook for a further 30 seconds.
2 Add 125 ml (1/2 cup) water, the tomato and sugar. Season. Bring to the boil. Reduce the heat and simmer for 10 minutes, or until reduced slightly.
3 Add the beans and parsley and simmer for a further 10 minutes, or until the beans are tender and the tomato mixture is pulpy. Season with salt and black pepper, and serve immediately as a side dish.

NUTRITION PER SERVE
Protein 5.5 g; Fat 20 g; Carbohydrate 9.5 g; Dietary Fibre 7.5 g; Cholesterol 0 mg; 992 kJ (237 Cal)

Using a sharp knife, finely chop the garlic cloves.

Cook the chopped onion in the olive oil until softened.

Simmer the tomato mixture until reduced slightly.

STUFFED CAPSICUM

Preparation time: 20 minutes
Total cooking time: 40 minutes
Serves 4

80 ml (1/3 cup) olive oil
125 g (2/3 cup) couscous
15 g (1/2 oz) butter
4 large red or yellow capsicums
   (peppers)
3 tablespoons pine nuts
1 onion, finely chopped
2 teaspoons ground cumin
1 teaspoon ground coriander
75 g (2 1/2 oz) raisins
3 tablespoons chopped fresh mint
2 tablespoons chopped fresh
   coriander (cilantro) leaves

Yoghurt dressing
250 g (1 cup) Greek-style plain
   yoghurt
2 tablespoons chopped fresh mint

1 Place 250 ml (1 cup) water in a
saucepan and bring to the boil. Add
1 tablespoon of the oil, a pinch of salt
and the couscous. Remove from the
heat and leave for 2 minutes, or until
the couscous is tender and has
absorbed all the liquid. Stir in the
butter with a fork and cook over low
heat for 3 minutes.
2 Preheat the oven to 190°C (375°F/
Gas 5). Grease a baking tray. Slice the
tops off the capsicums and remove
the seeds and membrane, reserving
the tops. Plunge the capsicums into
a saucepan of boiling water for
2 minutes; drain on paper towels.
3 Heat a frying pan over high heat.
Add the pine nuts and dry-fry for
2–3 minutes, or until golden brown.
Remove the pine nuts from the pan.
Heat 1 tablespoon of the olive oil in
the pan, add the onion and cook over
medium heat for 5 minutes, or until
softened. Add the cumin and
coriander, and cook for 1 minute.
Remove from the heat and stir into
the couscous with the pine nuts,
raisins and herbs, and season well.
4 Fill each capsicum with some of
the couscous stuffing and place on
the tray. Drizzle the remaining olive
oil over the capsicums and replace
the lids. Bake for 20–25 minutes, or

until tender. Meanwhile, combine
the yoghurt and mint, and place in
a serving dish. Serve the capsicums
with the dressing and a salad.

NUTRITION PER SERVE
Protein 6.5 g; Fat 25 g; Carbohydrate 28 g;
Dietary Fibre 3.5 g; Cholesterol 20 mg;
1500 kJ (560 Cal)

*Add the butter to the couscous and cook
for 3 minutes.*

*Spoon the couscous mixture into the
capsicum shells.*

OKRA IN TOMATO SAUCE AND CORIANDER

Preparation time: 5 minutes
Total cooking time: 15 minutes
Serves 4–6

60 ml (¼ cup) olive oil
1 onion, chopped
2 garlic cloves, crushed
500 g (1 lb 2 oz) fresh okra (see Note)

425 g (15 oz) can chopped tomatoes
2 teaspoons sugar
60 ml (¼ cup) lemon juice
55 g (1¾ cups) fresh coriander
   (cilantro) leaves, finely chopped

1 Heat the oil in a large frying pan, add the onion and cook over medium heat for 4 minutes, or until transparent and golden. Add the garlic and cook for a further minute.
2 Add the okra and cook, stirring, for 4–5 minutes. Add the tomato, sugar and juice, and simmer, stirring occasionally, for 3–4 minutes, or until softened. Stir in the coriander, remove from the heat and serve.

NUTRITION PER SERVE (6)
Protein 3.5 g; Fat 10 g; Carbohydrate 5.5 g; Dietary Fibre 4 g; Cholesterol 0 mg; 522 kJ (125 Cal)

COOK'S FILE
Note: If fresh okra is not available, use canned (800 g/1 lb 12 oz). Rinse and drain before adding with the coriander.

Add the garlic to the onion and cook for a further minute.

Stir the okra into the onion mixture and simmer for a few minutes.

Stir in the tomato, sugar and lemon juice and simmer until softened.

PAPPA AL POMADORO
(Tomato bread soup)

Preparation time: 20 minutes
+ 5 minutes standing
Total cooking time: 25 minutes
Serves 4

750 g (1 lb 10 oz) vine-ripened
   tomatoes
1 loaf (450 g/1 lb) day-old crusty
   Italian bread
1 tablespoon olive oil
3 garlic cloves, crushed
1 tablespoon tomato paste (purée)
1.25 litres (5 cups) hot vegetable stock
4 tablespoons torn fresh basil leaves
2–3 tablespoons extra virgin olive oil
extra virgin olive oil, extra, to serve

1 Score a cross in the base of each tomato. Place in a bowl of boiling water for 1 minute, then plunge into cold water and peel the skin away from the cross. Cut the tomatoes in half and scoop out the seeds with a teaspoon. Chop the tomato flesh.
2 Remove most of the crust from the bread and discard. Cut the bread into 3 cm (1¼ inch) pieces.
3 Heat the oil in a large saucepan. Add the garlic, tomato and tomato paste, then reduce the heat and simmer, stirring occasionally, for 10–15 minutes, or until reduced and thickened. Add the stock and bring to the boil, stirring for 2–3 minutes. Reduce the heat to medium, add the bread pieces and cook, stirring, for 5 minutes, or until the bread softens and absorbs most of the liquid. Add more stock or water if necessary.
4 Stir in the torn basil leaves and extra virgin olive oil, and leave for

5 minutes so the flavours have time to develop. Drizzle with a little extra virgin olive oil.

NUTRITION PER SERVE
Protein 12 g; Fat 22 g; Carbohydrate 58 g;
Dietary Fibre 6 g; Cholesterol 0 mg;
2008 kJ (480 Cal)

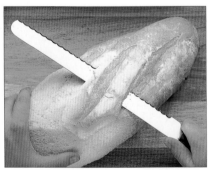

Remove most of the crust from the loaf of bread and discard.

Reduce the heat and simmer for 15 minutes, or until reduced.

Add the bread pieces to the tomato mixture and cook, stirring.

RED GAZPACHO
(Cold tomato soup)

Preparation time: 40 minutes
+ 5 minutes soaking
+ 2 hours refrigeration
Total cooking time: Nil
Serves 4

1 kg (2 lb 4 oz) vine-ripened tomatoes
2 slices day-old white Italian bread,
   crust removed, broken into pieces
1 red capsicum (pepper), seeded and
   roughly chopped
2 garlic cloves, chopped
1 small green chilli, chopped, optional
1 teaspoon sugar
2 tablespoons red wine vinegar
2 tablespoons extra virgin olive oil
8 ice cubes

Garnish
1/2 Lebanese (short) cucumber,
   seeded and finely diced
1/2 red capsicum (pepper), seeded
   and finely diced
1/2 green capsicum (pepper), seeded
   and finely diced
1/2 red onion, finely diced
1/2 tomato, diced

1 Score a cross in the base of each tomato. Place in a bowl of boiling water for 1 minute, then plunge into cold water and peel away from the cross. Cut the tomatoes in half, scoop out the seeds and chop the flesh.
2 Soak the bread in cold water for 5 minutes, then squeeze out any excess liquid. Place the bread in a food processor with the tomato, capsicum, garlic, chilli, sugar and vinegar, and process until smooth.
3 With the motor running, add the oil to make a smooth mixture. Season with salt and ground black pepper. Refrigerate for at least 2 hours. Add a little extra vinegar, if desired.
4 To make the garnish, place all the ingredients in a bowl and mix well. Serve the soup in bowls with 2 ice cubes in each bowl. Spoon the garnish into separate bowls.

NUTRITION PER SERVE
Protein 5.5 g; Fat 10 g; Carbohydrate 16 g;
Dietary Fibre 5 g; Cholesterol 0 mg;
760 kJ (180 Cal)

Soak the bread in water, then squeeze out any excess liquid.

Process the bread, tomato, capsicum, garlic, chilli, sugar and vinegar.

Place the garnish ingredients in a bowl and mix together well.

CHICKPEA SOUP

Preparation time: 15 minutes
  + overnight soaking
Total cooking time:
  1 hour 30 minutes
Serves 4

330 g (1 1/2 cups) dried chickpeas
1/2 brown onion
1 bay leaf
1/2 head (8 cloves) garlic, unpeeled
2 tablespoons olive oil
1 celery stick, chopped
1 large onion, extra, finely chopped
3 garlic cloves, extra, chopped
1 teaspoon ground cumin

1 teaspoon paprika
1/4 teaspoon dried chilli powder
3 teaspoons chopped fresh oregano
1 litre (4 cups) vegetable stock
2 tablespoons lemon juice
olive oil, extra to drizzle

1 Place the chickpeas in a bowl and cover with water. Soak overnight, then drain. Transfer the chickpeas to a saucepan. Add the onion, bay leaf, garlic and 1.5 litres (6 cups) water. Bring to the boil, then reduce the heat and simmer for 55–60 minutes, or until the chickpeas are tender. Drain, reserving 500 ml (2 cups) cooking liquid. Discard the onion, bay leaf and garlic.
2 Heat the oil in the same saucepan,

add the celery and extra onion, and cook over medium heat for 5 minutes, or until golden. Add the extra garlic and cook for a further 1 minute. Add the cumin, paprika, chilli powder and 2 teaspoons of the oregano, and cook, stirring, for 1 minute. Return the chickpeas to the pan and stir to coat with the spices.
3 Pour in the vegetable stock and reserved cooking liquid, bring to the boil, then reduce the heat and simmer for 20 minutes. Stir in the lemon juice and remaining oregano and serve drizzled with olive oil.

NUTRITION PER SERVE
Protein 16 g; Fat 20 g; Carbohydrate 34 g;
Dietary Fibre 12 g; Cholesterol 0 mg;
1565 kJ (374 Cal)

Cook the chickpeas, onion, bay leaf and garlic until the chickpeas are tender.

Add the cooked chickpeas to the pan and stir to coat with the spices.

Stir in the lemon juice and remaining fresh oregano.

AJO BLANCO
(White soup with garlic and grapes)

Preparation time: 20 minutes
+ 5 minutes soaking
+ refrigeration
Total cooking time: 3 minutes
Serves 4–6

1 loaf (200 g/7 oz) day-old white
  Italian bread, crust removed
155 g (1 cup) whole blanched
  almonds
3–4 garlic cloves, chopped
125 ml (1/2 cup) extra virgin
  olive oil
80 ml (1/3 cup) sherry vinegar or white
  wine vinegar

315–375 ml (1 1/4–1 1/2 cups) vegetable
  stock or water
2 tablespoons olive oil, extra
75 g (2 1/2 oz) day-old white Italian
  bread, extra, crust removed and
  cut into 1 cm (1/2 inch) cubes
200 g (7 oz) small seedless green
  grapes

1 Soak the bread in a bowl of cold water for 5 minutes, then squeeze to remove any excess moisture. Place the almonds and garlic in a food processor and process until well ground. Add the bread and process to a smooth paste.
2 With the motor running, add the oil in a slow steady stream until the mixture is the consistency of thick mayonnaise. Slowly add the sherry vinegar and 315 ml (1 1/4 cups) of

the stock, or water, until the mixture has reached the desired consistency. Blend for 1 minute. Season with salt, then refrigerate for at least 2 hours. The soup thickens on refrigeration so add more stock or water to reach the desired consistency.
3 Heat the extra olive oil in a large frying pan. Add the bread cubes and toss over medium heat for 2–3 minutes, or until evenly golden brown. Drain on crumpled paper towels. Serve the soup very cold garnished with the grapes and the bread cubes.

NUTRITION PER SERVE (6)
Protein 9.5 g; Fat 42 g; Carbohydrate 28 g;
Dietary Fibre 4 g; Cholesterol 0 mg;
2195 kJ (525 Cal)

Process the bread, almonds and garlic to a smooth paste.

Add the oil to the bread mixture until it resembles thick mayonnaise.

Pan-fry the bread cubes until they are evenly golden brown.

SEAFOOD

INSALATA DI FRUTTI DI MARE
(Seafood salad)

Preparation time: 45 minutes
 + 40 minutes marinating
Total cooking time: 10 minutes
Serves 4

500 g (1 lb 2 oz) small calamari
 (squid)
1 kg (2 lb 4 oz) large clams
1 kg (2 lb 4 oz) black mussels
500 g (1 lb 2 oz) raw medium prawns
 (shrimp), peeled and deveined,
 tails intact
5 tablespoons finely chopped fresh
 flat-leaf (Italian) parsley

Dressing
2 tablespoons lemon juice
80 ml (1/3 cup) olive oil
1 garlic clove, crushed

1 Grasp the body of the calamari in one hand and the head and tentacles in the other. Gently pull apart to separate. Cut the tentacles from the head by cutting below the eyes. Discard the head. Push out the beak and discard. Pull the quill from inside the body of the calamari and discard. Under cold running water, pull away all the skin (the flaps can be used). Rinse well, then slice the calamari into 7 mm (3/8 inch) rings.
2 Scrub the clams and mussels and remove the beards. Discard any that are cracked or don't close when tapped. Rinse under cold running water. Fill a large saucepan with 2 cm (3/4 inch) water, add the clams and mussels, cover, bring to the boil and cook for 4–5 minutes, or until the shells open. Remove, reserving the liquid. Discard any that do not open. Remove the mussels and clams from their shells and place in a large bowl.
3 Pour 1 litre (4 cups) water into the pan, bring to the boil and add the prawns and calamari. Cook for 3–4 minutes, or until the prawns turn pink and the calamari is tender. Drain and add to the clams and mussels.
4 To make the dressing, combine the lemon juice, olive oil and garlic in a small bowl and whisk together. Season with salt and freshly ground black pepper. Pour the dressing over the seafood, add 4 tablespoons of the parsley and toss to coat. Adjust the seasoning if necessary. Cover and marinate in the refrigerator for 30–40 minutes to allow the flavours to develop. Sprinkle with the remaining parsley and serve with slices of fresh crusty bread.

NUTRITION PER SERVE
Protein 76 g; Fat 25 g; Carbohydrate 2 g;
Dietary Fibre 0 g; Cholesterol 550 mg;
3420 kJ (815 Cal)

Remove the transparent quill from inside the body of the calamari.

Gently pull the mussels and clams out of their shells.

TUNA AND WHITE BEAN SALAD

Preparation time: 25 minutes
Total cooking time: 5 minutes
Serves 4–6

400 g (14 oz) tuna steaks
1 small red onion, thinly sliced
1 tomato, seeded and chopped
1 small red capsicum (pepper), thinly sliced
2 x 400 g (14 oz) cans cannellini beans
2 garlic cloves, crushed
1 teaspoon chopped fresh thyme
4 tablespoons finely chopped fresh flat-leaf (Italian) parsley
1½ tablespoons lemon juice
80 ml (⅓ cup) extra virgin olive oil
1 teaspoon honey
olive oil, for brushing
100 g (3½ oz) rocket (arugula) leaves
1 teaspoon lemon zest

1 Place the tuna on a plate; sprinkle with pepper on both sides. Cover with plastic and chill until needed.
2 Combine the onion, tomato and capsicum in a bowl. Rinse the beans under running water for 30 seconds, drain. Add to the bowl with the garlic, thyme and 3 tablespoons of parsley.
3 Place the lemon juice, oil and honey in a small saucepan, bring to the boil, then simmer, stirring, for 1 minute, or until the honey dissolves. Remove from the heat.
4 Brush a barbecue or chargrill with olive oil, and heat until very hot. Cook the tuna for 1 minute on each side. The meat should still be pink in the middle. Slice into 3 cm (1¼ inch) cubes and combine with the salad. Pour on the dressing and toss well.
5 Place the rocket on a platter. Top with the salad, season and garnish with the zest and parsley. Serve.

NUTRITION PER SERVE (6)
Protein 30 g; Fat 20 g; Carbohydrate 17 g; Dietary Fibre 10 g; Cholesterol 0 mg; 1656 kJ (394 Cal)

Add the beans, garlic, thyme and parsley to the bowl and mix well.

Heat the lemon juice, honey and oil in a saucepan until the honey dissolves.

Cook the tuna until still pink in the middle, and cut into 3 cm (1¼ inch) cubes.

INVOLTINI OF SWORDFISH

Preparation time: 30 minutes
Total cooking time: 10 minutes
Serves 4

1 kg (2 lb 4 oz) swordfish, skin
   removed, cut into four 5 cm
   (2 inch) pieces
3 lemons
80 ml (1/3 cup) olive oil
1 small onion, chopped
3 garlic cloves, chopped
2 tablespoons chopped capers
2 tablespoons chopped pitted
   Kalamata olives
35 g (1/3 cup) finely grated Parmesan
   cheese
120 g (11/2 cups) fresh breadcrumbs
2 tablespoons chopped fresh parsley
1 egg, lightly beaten
24 fresh bay leaves
2 small white onions, quartered and
   separated into pieces
2 tablespoons lemon juice, extra

1 Cut each swordfish piece
horizontally into 4 slices to give you
16 slices. Place each piece between
two pieces of plastic wrap and roll
gently with a rolling pin to flatten
without tearing. Cut each piece in
half to give 32 pieces.
2 Peel the lemons with a vegetable
peeler; cut the peel into 24 pieces.
Juice the lemon to give 60 ml (1/4 cup).
3 Heat 2 tablespoons olive oil, add
the onion and garlic, and cook over
medium heat for 2 minutes. Place
in a bowl with the capers, olives,
Parmesan, breadcrumbs and parsley.
Season, add the egg and mix to bind.
4 Divide the stuffing among the fish
pieces and, with oiled hands, roll up

to form parcels. Thread 4 rolls onto
each of 8 skewers, alternating with
the bay leaves, lemon peel and onion.
5 Mix the remaining oil and the
lemon juice. Barbecue or grill (broil)
the skewers for 3–4 minutes each side,

basting with the oil and lemon mix.
Drizzle with extra lemon juice.

NUTRITION PER SERVE
Protein 34 g; Fat 38 g; Carbohydrate 5.5 g;
Dietary Fibre 5 g; Cholesterol 193 mg;
2065 kJ (493 Cal)

*Roll the swordfish out between two pieces
of plastic wrap.*

*Roll the fish pieces and filling up to form
neat parcels.*

*Thread the rolls, bay leaves, lemon peel
and onion onto skewers.*

TUNA SKEWERS WITH MOROCCAN SPICES AND CHERMOULA

Preparation time: 20 minutes
  + 10 minutes marinating
Total cooking time: 5 minutes
Serves 4

800 g (1 lb 12 oz) tuna steaks, cut
  into 3 cm (1¼ inch) cubes
2 tablespoons olive oil
½ teaspoon ground cumin
2 teaspoons grated lemon zest

Chermoula
3 teaspoons ground cumin
½ teaspoon ground coriander
2 teaspoons paprika
pinch cayenne pepper
4 garlic cloves, crushed
15 g (½ cup) chopped fresh flat-leaf
  (Italian) parsley
25 g (½ cup) chopped fresh
  coriander (cilantro)
80 ml (⅓ cup) lemon juice
125 ml (½ cup) olive oil

1 If using wooden skewers, soak for 30 minutes to prevent burning. Place the tuna in a shallow non-metallic dish. Combine the olive oil, ground cumin and lemon zest, and pour over the tuna. Toss to coat and leave to marinate for 10 minutes.
2 To make the chermoula, place the cumin, coriander, paprika and cayenne in a frying pan and cook over medium heat for 30 seconds, or until fragrant. Combine with the remaining ingredients and leave for the flavours to develop.
3 Thread the tuna onto the skewers. Lightly oil a chargrill (griddle) or barbecue, and cook the skewers for 1 minute on each side for rare and 2 minutes for medium. Serve on couscous with the chermoula drizzled over the skewers.

NUTRITION PER SERVE
Protein 50 g; Fat 40 g; Carbohydrate 0 g;
Dietary Fibre 0 g; Cholesterol 70 mg;
2186 kJ (520 Cal)

Pour the combined olive oil, cumin and lemon zest over the tuna cubes.

Combine the chermoula ingredients in a small bowl.

Thread the tuna onto the skewers and grill (broil) until done to your liking.

SALAD NICOISE

Preparation time: 30 minutes
Total cooking time: 15 minutes
Serves 4

3 eggs
2 vine-ripened tomatoes
175 g (6 oz) baby green beans,
   trimmed
125 ml (1/2 cup) olive oil
2 tablespoons white wine vinegar
1 large garlic clove, halved
325 g (11 1/2 oz) iceberg lettuce heart,
   cut into 8 wedges
1 small red capsicum (pepper),
   seeded and thinly sliced
1 celery stick, cut into 5 cm (2 inch)
   thin strips

1 Lebanese (short) cucumber, cut into
   thin 5 cm (2 inch) lengths
1/4 large red onion, thinly sliced
2 x 185 g (6 3/4 oz) cans tuna, drained,
   broken into chunks
12 Kalamata olives
45 g (1 1/2 oz) can anchovy fillets,
   drained
2 teaspoons baby capers
12 small fresh basil leaves

1 Place the eggs in a saucepan of cold water. Bring slowly to the boil, then reduce the heat and simmer for 10 minutes. Stir during the first few minutes to centre the yolks. Cool under cold water, then peel and cut into quarters. Meanwhile, score a cross in the base of each tomato. Place in boiling water for 1 minute, then plunge into cold water; peel the skin

away from the cross. Cut into eighths.
2 Cook the beans in a saucepan of boiling water for 2 minutes, then refresh quickly under cold water and drain. Place the oil and vinegar in a jar and shake to combine.
3 Rub the garlic halves over the base and sides of a large salad serving platter. Arrange the lettuce wedges evenly over the base. Layer the tomato, capsicum, celery, cucumber, beans and egg quarters over the lettuce. Scatter with the onion and tuna. Arrange the olives, anchovies, capers and basil leaves over the top, pour the dressing over the salad and serve immediately.

NUTRITION PER SERVE
Protein 63 g; Fat 32 g; Carbohydrate 25 g;
Dietary Fibre 5 g; Cholesterol 228 mg;
2697 kJ (644 Cal)

Using a sharp knife, cut the celery stick into long, thin strips.

Cut the peeled tomatoes into quarters, and again into eighths.

Layer the tomato, capsicum, celery, cucumber, beans and egg over the lettuce.

65

BOUILLABAISSE WITH ROUILLE
(French seafood soup with capsicum sauce)

Preparation time: 30 minutes
+ 5 minutes soaking
Total cooking time:
1 hour 15 minutes
Serves 6

500 g (1 lb 2 oz) ripe tomatoes
3 tablespoons olive oil
1 large onion, chopped
2 leeks, sliced
4 garlic cloves, crushed
1–2 tablespoons tomato paste (purée)
6 sprigs fresh flat-leaf (Italian) parsley
2 bay leaves
2 sprigs fresh thyme
1 sprig fresh fennel
1/4 teaspoon saffron threads
2 kg (2 lb 4 oz) seafood trimmings,
    e.g. fish heads, bones, shellfish
    remains
1 tablespoon Pernod or Ricard
4 potatoes, cut into 1.5 cm (5/8 inch)
    slices
1.5 kg (3 lb 5 oz) fish fillets and
    steaks, such as snapper, red fish,
    blue eye and bream, cut into large
    chunks (see Note)
2 tablespoons chopped fresh
    flat-leaf (Italian) parsley

Toasts

1/2 baguette, cut into twelve
    1.5 cm (5/8 inch) slices
2 large garlic cloves, halved

Rouille

3 slices day-old Italian white bread,
    crusts removed
1 red capsicum (pepper), seeded,
    quartered
1 small red chilli, seeded, chopped
3 garlic cloves, crushed
1 tablespoon chopped fresh basil
80 ml (1/3 cup) olive oil

1 Score a cross in the base of each
tomato. Place the tomatoes in a bowl
of boiling water for 1 minute, then
plunge into cold water and peel the
skin away from the cross. Roughly
chop the tomatoes.
2 Heat the oil in a large saucepan
over low heat, add the onion and leek
and cook for 5 minutes without
browning. Add the garlic, tomato and
1 tablespoon tomato paste, and
simmer for 5 minutes. Stir in 2 litres
(8 cups) cold water, then add the
parsley, bay leaves, thyme, fennel,
saffron and seafood trimmings. Bring
to the boil, then reduce the heat and
simmer for 30–40 minutes.
3 Strain into a large saucepan,
pressing the juices out of the
ingredients. Set aside 60 ml (1/4 cup)
stock. Add the Pernod to the pan and
stir in extra tomato paste if needed to
enrich the colour. Season. Bring to
the boil, add the potato, then reduce
the heat and simmer for 5 minutes.
4 Add the blue-eye and bream and
cook for 2–3 minutes, then add the
red fish and snapper, and cook for
5–6 minutes, or until cooked.
5 To make the toasts, toast the bread
until golden on both sides. While
still warm, rub with the garlic.
6 To make the rouille, soak the
bread, in enough cold water to cover,
for 5 minutes. Cook the capsicum,
skin-side-up, under a hot grill (broiler)
until the skin blackens and blisters.
Place in a plastic bag and leave to
cool, then peel away the skin.
Roughly chop the flesh. Squeeze the
bread dry and place in a food
processor with the capsicum, chilli,
garlic and basil. Process to a smooth
paste. With the motor running,
gradually add the oil until the
consistency resembles mayonnaise.
Thin the sauce with 1–2 tablespoons
of the reserved fish stock. Season
with salt and ground black pepper.
7 To serve, place 2 pieces of toast
in the base of six soup bowls. Spoon
in the soup and fish pieces and
scatter some parsley over the top.
Serve with the rouille.

NUTRITION PER SERVE
Protein 60 g; Fat 30 g; Carbohydrate 40 g;
Dietary Fibre 5.5 g; Cholesterol 175 mg;
2838 kJ (678 Cal)

COOK'S FILE
Note: It is important to try to use at least
four different varieties of fish, choosing a
range of textures and flavours.
Rascasse, where available, is traditional,
but cod, bass, John dory, halibut,
monkfish, turbot, hake and red mullet
are also used. Shellfish such as lobster,
scallops or mussels can be used.

*Simmer the onion, leek, garlic, tomato
and tomato paste for 5 minutes.*

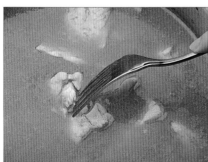

Cook the firmer-fleshed fish pieces slightly longer than the delicate pieces.

Rub the halved garlic cloves over the toasted bread.

Process the rouille to the consistency of mayonnaise.

SPAGHETTI WITH OLIVE, CAPER AND ANCHOVY SAUCE

Preparation time: 15 minutes
Total cooking time: 20 minutes
Serves 6

375 g (13 oz) spaghetti
80 ml (1/3 cup) olive oil
2 onions, finely chopped
3 garlic cloves, finely chopped
1/2 teaspoon chilli flakes

6 large ripe tomatoes, diced
4 tablespoons capers in brine, rinsed, drained
7–8 anchovies in oil, drained, minced
150 g (5½ oz) Kalamata olives
3 tablespoons chopped fresh flat-leaf (Italian) parsley

1 Bring a large saucepan of salted water to the boil, add the spaghetti and cook until *al dente*. Drain.
2 Meanwhile, heat the oil in a saucepan, add the onion and cook over medium heat for 5 minutes. Add the garlic and chilli flakes, and cook for 30 seconds, then add the tomato, capers and anchovies. Simmer over low heat for 5–10 minutes, or until thick and pulpy, then stir in the olives and parsley.
3 Stir the pasta through the sauce. Season with salt and freshly ground black pepper and serve immediately with crusty bread.

NUTRITION PER SERVE
Protein 10 g; Fat 15 g; Carbohydrate 49 g; Dietary Fibre 6.5 g; Cholesterol 2 mg; 1563 kJ (373 Cal)

Mince the drained anchovies in a mortar and pestle.

Cook the spaghetti in a pan of lightly salted boiling water until al dente.

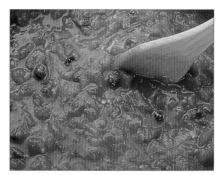

Simmer the tomato and caper mixture over low heat until thick and pulpy.

CAPONATA WITH CHARGRILLED TUNA

Preparation time: 25 minutes
+ 1 hour standing + cooling
Total cooking time: 50 minutes
Serves 6

Caponata
500 g (1 lb 2 oz) ripe tomatoes
750 g (1 lb 10 oz) eggplant, cut into
　1 cm (1/2 inch) cubes
80 ml (1/3 cup) olive oil
2 tablespoons olive oil, extra
1 onion, chopped
3 celery sticks, chopped
2 tablespoons drained capers
90 g (1/2 cup) green olives, pitted
1 tablespoon sugar
125 ml (1/2 cup) red wine vinegar

olive oil, for brushing
6 x 200 g (7 oz) tuna steaks

1 To make the caponata, score a cross in the base of each tomato. Place in a bowl of boiling water for 1 minute, then plunge into cold water and peel away from the cross. Cut into 1 cm (1/2 inch) cubes.
2 Sprinkle the eggplant with salt and leave for 1 hour. Place in a colander, rinse under cold running water and pat dry. Heat half the oil in a frying pan, add half the eggplant and cook for 4–5 minutes, or until golden and soft. Remove. Repeat with the remaining oil and eggplant. Remove.
3 Heat the extra oil in the same pan, add the onion and celery, and cook for 3–4 minutes, or until golden. Reduce the heat to low, add the tomato and simmer for 15 minutes, stirring occasionally. Stir in the capers, olives, sugar and vinegar, season and simmer, stirring occasionally, for 10 minutes, or until slightly reduced. Stir in the eggplant. Remove from the heat and cool.
4 Heat a chargrill plate (griddle) and brush lightly with olive oil. Cook the tuna for 2–3 minutes each side, or until cooked to your liking. Serve immediately with the caponata.

NUTRITION PER SERVE
Protein 45 g; Fat 30 g; Carbohydrate 7 g; Dietary Fibre 5 g; Cholesterol 140 mg; 1963 kJ (470 Cal)

Cook the eggplant in two batches until golden and soft.

Add the capers, olives, sugar and vinegar to the tomato mixture.

Cook the tuna on a chargrill plate (griddle) until cooked to your liking.

MUSSELS IN TOMATO AND HERB SAUCE

Preparation time: 30 minutes
Total cooking time: 35 minutes
Serves 4

Tomato and herb sauce
80 ml (¹/₃ cup) olive oil
3 garlic cloves, finely chopped
¹/₄ teaspoon dried chilli flakes
2 x 425 g (15 oz) cans crushed
    tomatoes
1 teaspoon caster (superfine) sugar

8 slices crusty Italian bread
2 tablespoons olive oil
2 large garlic cloves, halved
1 kg (2 lb 4 oz) black mussels
2 tablespoons olive oil, extra
1 red onion, finely chopped
6 sprigs fresh flat-leaf parsley
2 sprigs fresh thyme
2 sprigs fresh oregano
250 ml (1 cup) dry white wine
1 tablespoon chopped fresh flat-leaf
    (Italian) parsley
2 teaspoons fresh thyme leaves
2 teaspoons chopped fresh oregano
    leaves

1 Preheat the oven to 160°C (315°F/ Gas 2–3). To make the tomato sauce, heat the oil in a saucepan, add the garlic and chilli flakes, and cook over low heat for 30 seconds without browning. Add the tomato, sugar and 80 ml (¹/₃ cup) water. Season and simmer, stirring often, for 15 minutes, or until reduced and thickened.
2 Lightly brush the bread with olive oil. Place in a single layer on a baking tray and bake for 10 minutes, or until crisp and golden. While still warm, rub one side with the garlic.
3 Meanwhile, scrub the mussels with a stiff brush and pull out the hairy beards. Discard any broken mussels or ones that don't close when tapped on the bench. Rinse well.
4 Heat the extra oil in a large saucepan, add the onion and cook over medium heat for 3 minutes, or until softened but not browned. Add the parsley, thyme, oregano and wine. Bring to the boil, then reduce the heat and simmer for 5 minutes. Season with pepper.

5 Add the mussels, stir to coat, and cook, covered, for 3–4 minutes. Shake the pan often. Remove the mussels as they open. Discard any unopened mussels.
6 Strain the wine mixture into the tomato sauce, discarding the onion and herbs. Return to the large saucepan and reheat. Add the

mussels and toss well to coat in the mixture. Pile into a serving bowl and scatter with the chopped parsley, thyme and oregano. Arrange the bread slices around the bowl.

NUTRITION PER SERVE
Protein 19 g; Fat 31.5 g; Carbohydrate 43 g; Dietary Fibre 6 g; Cholesterol 41.5 mg; 2385 kJ (570 Cal)

Pull the hairy beards out of the scrubbed mussels.

Remove the mussels as they open and discard any that don't open.

PISSALADIERE
(Provençal onion tart)

Preparation time: 30 minutes
+ 15 minutes standing
+ 1 hour 30 minutes rising
Total cooking time:
1 hour 25 minutes
Serves 4–6

7 g (¼ oz) sachet dry yeast
175 g (1¼ cup) plain (all-purpose) flour
1 egg, beaten
1 tablespoon olive oil

Topping
60 ml (¼ cup) olive oil
2 garlic cloves
1 sprig fresh thyme
4 large onions (800 g/1 lb 12 oz),
thinly sliced
pinch ground nutmeg
30 g (1 oz) drained anchovy fillets,
halved lengthways
16 pitted black olives

1 Place the yeast in a bowl with 2 tablespoons lukewarm water. Leave in a warm place for 15 minutes, or until foamy.
2 Sift the flour and ¼ teaspoon salt into a large bowl, make a well in the centre and add the yeast mixture, egg, oil and 2 tablespoons warm water. Bring together with a wooden spoon and when clumped together, transfer to a lightly floured surface. Knead to a soft, pliable dough, adding a little more water or flour as needed. Continue kneading for 6–8 minutes, or until smooth and elastic. Lightly oil a clean large bowl and place the dough in it. Roll the dough around to coat with oil, cover the bowl with a dry tea towel and place in a warm place for 1 hour, or until doubled in size.
3 To make the topping, heat the oil in a large frying pan, add the garlic, thyme and onion and cook, stirring occasionally, over low heat for 1 hour, or until the onion is soft and buttery but not brown. Discard the garlic and thyme, add the nutmeg and season.
4 Brush a 30 cm (12 inch) round pizza tray with oil. Punch down the dough and lightly knead into a ball. Roll out to a 30 cm (12 inch) circle and place over the oiled tray. Spread the onion over the surface, leaving a 1 cm (½ inch) border. Make a diamond cross-hatch pattern on top with the anchovies. Intersperse with the olives. Slide the tray into a large plastic bag and leave to rise again for 30 minutes. Preheat the oven to 200°C (400°F/Gas 6).

5 Bake for 20–25 minutes, or until the dough is cooked and golden. Reduce the heat to 190°C (375°F/Gas 5) if the crust overbrowns towards the end of baking. Serve in slices.

NUTRITION PER SERVE (6)
Protein 8 g; Fat 15 g; Carbohydrate 28 g; Dietary Fibre 4 g; Cholesterol 34 mg; 1153 kJ (275 Cal)

Using a rolling pin, roll the dough out to a 30 cm (12 inch) circle.

Arrange the anchovies and olives over the top of the onion mixture.

71

PSARI TAHINA
(Baked fish with tahini sauce)

Preparation time: 30 minutes
Total cooking time: 30 minutes
Serves 4

1 kg (2 lb 4 oz) whole white-fleshed
   fish, (snapper, bream or barramundi),
   scaled and cleaned
3 garlic cloves, crushed
2 teaspoons harissa
2 tablespoons olive oil
1 lemon, thinly sliced
1 onion, thinly sliced
2 large firm, ripe tomatoes, sliced
4 sprigs fresh thyme

Tahini sauce
2 teaspoons olive oil
1 garlic clove, crushed
3 tablespoons light tahini
2 1/2 tablespoons lemon juice
1 1/2 tablespoons chopped fresh
   coriander (cilantro) leaves

1 Preheat the oven to 200°C (400°F/
Gas 6). Lightly grease a large baking
dish. Make 3–4 diagonal cuts on each
side of the fish through the thickest
part of the flesh and to the bone to
ensure even cooking. Combine the
garlic, harissa and olive oil in a small
dish. Place 2 teaspoons in the cavity
and spread the remainder over both
sides of the fish, rubbing it into the
slits. Place 2 lemon slices in the cavity
of the fish.
2 Arrange the onion in a layer on the
baking dish. Top with the tomato,
thyme and remaining lemon slices.
Place the fish on top and bake,
uncovered, for about 25–30 minutes,
or until the fish flesh is opaque.

3 Meanwhile, to make the sauce,
heat the olive oil in a small saucepan
over low heat and cook the garlic
over medium heat for 30 seconds,
then stir in the tahini, lemon juice
and 125 ml (1/2 cup) water. Add more
water, if necessary, to make a smooth,
but fairly thick sauce. Cook for
2 minutes, then remove from the heat
and stir in the coriander. Season.

4 Transfer the onion and tomato to
a serving dish. Place the fish on top
and season with salt. Pour the sauce
into a dish and serve on the side.

NUTRITION PER SERVE
Protein 60 g; Fat 25 g; Carbohydrate 1 g;
Dietary Fibre 3 g; Cholesterol 192 mg;
2042 kJ (490 Cal)

*Spread the remaining harissa mixture
over the sides of the fish.*

*Bake the fish in a moderately hot oven
until the flesh is opaque.*

*Add some water to the tahini sauce, if
necessary, to make it smooth but thick.*

STUFFED SQUID

Preparation time: 50 minutes
Total cooking time: 50 minutes
Serves 4

500 g (1 lb 2 oz) firm ripe tomatoes
100 ml (3¹/₂ fl oz) olive oil
1 large onion, finely chopped
2 garlic cloves, crushed
160 g (1 cup) fresh breadcrumbs
1 egg, lightly beaten
60 g (2¹/₄ oz) kefalotyri cheese, grated
60 g (2¹/₄ oz) haloumi cheese, grated
4 large or 8 small squid (1 kg/2 lb 4 oz),
    cleaned (see Note)
1 small onion, finely chopped, extra
2 garlic cloves, crushed, extra
150 ml (5¹/₂ fl oz) good-quality red
    wine
1 tablespoon chopped fresh oregano
1 tablespoon chopped fresh flat-leaf
    (Italian) parsley

1 Score a cross in the base of each tomato. Place the tomatoes in a bowl of boiling water for 1 minute, then plunge into cold water and peel the skin from the cross. Dice the flesh.
2 Heat 2 tablespoons of the oil in a frying pan, add the onion and cook over medium heat for 3 minutes. Remove. Combine with the garlic, breadcrumbs, egg and cheese. Season.
3 Pat the squid hoods dry with paper towels and, using a teaspoon, fill three-quarters full with the stuffing. Do not pack too tightly or the mixture will swell and burst out during cooking. Secure with toothpicks.
4 Heat the remaining oil in a large frying pan, add the squid and cook for 1–2 minutes on all sides. Remove. Add the extra onion and cook over medium heat for 3 minutes, or until soft, then add the extra garlic and cook for a further 1 minute. Stir in the tomato and wine, and simmer for 10 minutes, or until thick and pulpy, then stir in the herbs. Return the squid to the pan and cook, covered, for 20–25 minutes, or until tender. Serve warm with the tomato sauce or cool with a salad.

NUTRITION PER SERVE
Protein 57 g; Fat 35 g; Carbohydrate 30 g; Dietary Fibre 4 g; Cholesterol 558 mg; 2890 kJ (690 Cal)

COOK'S FILE
Note: Ask the fishmonger to clean the squid. Or, discard the tentacles and cartilage. Rinse the hoods under running water and pull off the skin.

Fill the squid tubes three-quarters full with the stuffing.

Cook the stuffed squid tubes on all sides in a frying pan.

Add the squid to the tomato mixture and cook until tender.

CALZONE WITH OLIVES, CAPERS AND ANCHOVIES

Preparation time: 35 minutes
+ 1 hour 45 minutes rising
Total cooking time: 15 minutes
Serves 4

1 tablespoon caster (superfine) sugar
7 g (1/4 oz) sachet dry yeast
540 g (4 1/3 cups) plain (all-purpose) flour
3 tablespoons olive oil
polenta, for dusting

Filling

2 tablespoons olive oil
200 g (7 oz) mozzarella cheese, cut into 1 cm (1/2 inch) cubes
2 medium tomatoes, juice squeezed out and cut into 1 cm (1/2 inch) dice
12 basil leaves, torn into pieces
20 pitted black olives
2 teaspoons baby capers
12 anchovy fillets, cut into thin strips 2 cm (3/4 inch) long

1 Place the sugar, yeast and 80 ml (1/3 cup) warm water in a small bowl. Leave in a warm place for 15 minutes, or until foamy. If it does not foam in 5 minutes the yeast is dead and you must start again.
2 Sift the flour into a large bowl with 1/2 teaspoon salt. Add the yeast mixture, olive oil and 170 ml (2/3 cup) warm water. Mix with a wooden spoon until the dough loosely clumps together. Turn it out onto a lightly floured surface and knead to form a soft, moist but non-sticky dough. Add a little extra flour or warm water as needed. Knead for 15–20 minutes, or until smooth and elastic, and a

finger imprint springs straight out.
3 Oil the sides of a large bowl with olive oil. Roll the ball of dough around in the bowl to coat the surface with oil, then cut a shallow cross on the top of the ball with a sharp knife. Cover the bowl with a tea towel and leave in a warm place for up to 1 hour 30 minutes, or until the dough has doubled in size.
4 Preheat the oven to 230°C (450°F/ Gas 8). Lightly oil 2 pizza or baking trays and dust with polenta. Punch down the dough. Place it on a lightly floured work surface and divide into two portions. One or both portions can be frozen at this stage for future use. Shape one portion into a ball. Roll it out to a circle of roughly 25 cm (10 inch). Using the heels of your hands and working from the centre outwards, press the circle to a diameter of 32 cm (13 inch). Transfer to the tray. Brush the surface lightly with olive oil.
5 Scatter half the mozzarella over one half of the dough, leaving a 1 cm (1/2 inch) border at the outer edge. Scatter half the tomato and basil over the cheese. Season. Distribute half the olives, capers and anchovies over the top. Fold the undressed half of dough over the filling to form a half-moon shape. Press together firmly to seal. Turn the cut edge up and over on itself and press into a scroll pattern to further seal in the filling. Brush the surface with a little more olive oil. Repeat with the remaining ingredients to make a second calzone. Bake for 10–15 minutes, or until puffed and golden brown.

NUTRITION PER SERVE
Protein 30 g; Fat 37 g; Carbohydrate 100 g; Dietary Fibre 6.5 g; Cholesterol 34 mg; 3679 kJ (880 Cal)

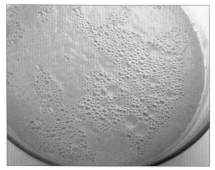

Leave the yeast, sugar and water mixture in a warm place until foamy.

Knead the dough to form a soft, moist but non-sticky dough.

Place the dough on a lightly floured work surface and divide in half.

Press the dough out to a 32 cm (13 inch) circle using the heels of your hands.

Distribute half the filling ingredients over the dough.

Press the edges together in a scroll pattern to fully seal.

ZARZUELA DE PESCADO
(Catalan fish stew)

Preparation time: 30 minutes
Total cooking time: 40 minutes
Serves 6–8

300 g (10½ oz) red mullet fillets
400 g (14 oz) firm white fish fillets
300 g (10½ oz) cleaned calamari
   (squid)
1.5 litres (6 cups) fish stock
80 ml (⅓ cup) olive oil
1 onion, chopped
6 garlic cloves, chopped
1 small red chilli, chopped
1 teaspoon paprika
pinch saffron threads
150 ml (5 fl oz) white wine
425 g (15 oz) can crushed tomatoes
16 raw medium prawns (shrimp),
   peeled, deveined, tails intact
2 tablespoons brandy
24 black mussels, cleaned
1 tablespoon chopped fresh parsley

Picada
2 tablespoons olive oil
2 slices day-old bread, cubed
2 garlic cloves
5 blanched almonds, toasted
2 tablespoons fresh flat-leaf (Italian)
   parsley

1 Cut the fish and calamari into 4 cm (1½ inch) pieces. Place the stock in a large pan, bring to the boil and boil for 15 minutes, or until reduced by half.
2 To make the picada, heat the oil in a frying pan, cook the bread, stirring, for 2–3 minutes, or until golden, adding the garlic for the last minute. Place the nuts, bread, garlic and parsley in a food processor and process. Add enough stock for a smooth paste.
3 Heat 2 tablespoons of the oil in a large saucepan, add the onion, garlic, chilli and paprika, and cook, stirring, for 1 minute. Add the saffron, wine, tomatoes and stock. Bring to the boil, then reduce the heat and simmer.
4 Heat the remaining oil in a frying pan and quickly fry the fish and calamari for 3–5 minutes. Remove from the pan. Add the prawns, cook for 1 minute , then pour in the brandy. Carefully ignite the brandy with a match and let the flames burn down. Remove from the pan.
5 Add the mussels to the stock and simmer, covered, for 2–3 minutes, or until opened—discard any unopened. Add all the seafood and the picada to the pan, stirring until the sauce has thickened and the seafood is cooked. Season. Sprinkle with parsley; serve.

NUTRITION PER SERVE (8)
Protein 26 g; Fat 18 g; Carbohydrate 5 g;
Dietary Fibre 1.5 g; Cholesterol 136 mg;
1275 kJ (305 Cal)

Process the nuts, bread, garlic, parsley and stock to a smooth paste.

Quickly cook the fish and calamari in a frying pan.

Add the mussels to the stock and simmer until they open.

OKTAPODI KRASATO
(Greek octopus in red wine stew)

Preparation time: 25 minutes
Total cooking time:
  1 hour 10 minutes
Serves 4–6

1 kg (2 lb 4 oz) baby octopus
2 tablespoons olive oil
1 large onion, chopped
3 garlic cloves, crushed
1 bay leaf
750 ml (3 cups) red wine
60 ml (¼ cup) red wine vinegar
400 g (14 oz) can crushed tomatoes
1 tablespoon tomato paste (purée)
1 tablespoon chopped fresh oregano
¼ teaspoon ground cinnamon
small pinch ground cloves
1 teaspoon sugar
2 tablespoons finely chopped fresh
   flat-leaf (Italian) parsley

1 Cut between the head and tentacles of the octopus, just below the eyes. Grasp the body and push the beak out and up through the centre of the tentacles with your fingers. Cut the eyes from the head by slicing a small round off. Discard the eye section. Carefully slit through one side, avoiding the ink sac, and remove any gut from inside. Rinse the octopus well under running water.

2 Heat the oil in a large saucepan, add the onion and cook over medium heat for 5 minutes, or until starting to brown. Add the garlic and bay leaf, and cook for 1 minute further. Add the octopus and stir to coat in the onion mixture.

3 Stir in the wine, vinegar, tomato, tomato paste, oregano, cinnamon, cloves and sugar. Bring to the boil, then reduce the heat and simmer for 1 hour, or until the octopus is tender and the sauce has thickened slightly. Stir in the parsley and season to taste with salt and ground black pepper. Serve with a Greek salad and crusty bread to mop up the delicious juices.

NUTRITION PER SERVE (6)
Protein 29 g; Fat 8.5 g; Carbohydrate 3.5 g; Dietary Fibre 1.5 g; Cholesterol 332 mg; 1234 kJ (295 Cal)

Cut between the head and the tentacles of the octopus.

Slit the head section and remove any gut from the inside.

Add the octopus to the pan and stir to coat in the onion mixture.

Simmer until the octopus is tender and the sauce has thickened slightly.

MEAT AND POULTRY

KHORESHE FESENJAN
(Duck breast with walnut and pomegranate sauce)

Preparation time: 15 minutes
+ 5 minutes resting
Total cooking time: 25 minutes
Serves 4

4 large duck breasts
1 onion, finely chopped
250 ml (1 cup) fresh pomegranate
    juice (see Note)
2 tablespoons lemon juice
2 tablespoons soft brown sugar
1 teaspoon ground cinnamon
185 g (1 1/2 cups) chopped
    walnuts
pomegranate seeds, to garnish,
    optional

1 Preheat the oven to 180°C (350°F/ Gas 4). Score the duck breasts 2 or 3 times with a sharp knife. Place in a non-stick frying pan and cook over high heat, skin-side down, for 6 minutes, or until crisp and it has rendered most of its fat. Place in a baking dish.
2 Remove all but 1 tablespoon of fat from the pan. Add the onion to the pan and cook over medium heat for 2–3 minutes, or until golden. Add the pomegranate and lemon juice, sugar, cinnamon and 125 g (1 cup) walnuts and cook for 1 minute. Pour over the duck breasts and bake for 15 minutes.
3 Leave the duck breasts to rest for 5 minutes while you skim any excess fat from the sauce. Slice the duck breasts and serve with a little of the sauce. Garnish with the pomegranate seeds and remaining walnuts, if desired.

NUTRITION PER SERVE
Protein 38 g; Fat 44 g; Carbohydrate 16 g; Dietary Fibre 3.5 g; Cholesterol 176.5 mg; 2535 kJ (605 Cal)

COOK'S FILE
Note: If fresh pomegranate juice is not available, combine 60 ml (1/4 cup) pomegranate concentrate with 185 ml (3/4 cup) water.

Score the duck breasts 2 or 3 times with a sharp knife.

Pour the pomegranate sauce over the duck breasts.

AVGOLEMONO WITH CHICKEN

Preparation time: 30 minutes
Total cooking time: 30 minutes
Serves 4

1 onion, halved
2 cloves
1 carrot, cut into chunks
1 bay leaf
500 g (1 lb 2 oz) chicken breast fillets
75 g (⅓ cup) short-grain rice
3 eggs, separated
3 tablespoons lemon juice
2 tablespoons chopped fresh
   flat-leaf (Italian) parsley
4 thin lemon slices, to garnish

1 Stud the onion halves with the cloves and place in a large saucepan with 1.5 litres (6 cups) water. Add the carrot, bay leaf and chicken. Season with salt and pepper. Slowly bring to the boil, then reduce the heat and simmer for 10 minutes, or until the chicken is cooked.
2 Strain the stock into a clean saucepan, reserving the chicken and discarding the vegetables. Add the rice to the stock, bring to the boil, then reduce the heat and simmer for 15 minutes, or until tender. Tear the chicken into shreds.
3 Whisk the egg whites until stiff peaks form, then beat in the yolks. Slowly beat in the lemon juice. Gently stir in 150 ml (5 fl oz) of the hot (not boiling) soup and beat thoroughly. Add the egg mixture to the soup and stir gently over low heat until thickened slightly. It should still be quite thin. Do not let it boil or the eggs may scramble. Add the shredded chicken and season.
4 Set aside for 3–4 minutes to allow the flavours to develop, then sprinkle the parsley over the top. Garnish with the lemon slices and serve.

NUTRITION PER SERVE
Protein 35 g; Fat 6.5 g; Carbohydrate 18 g; Dietary Fibre 1.5 g; Cholesterol 198 mg; 1145 kJ (274 Cal)

COOK'S FILE
Note: Avgolemono is a Greek soup made with egg and lemon. Serve immediately as it doesn't keep well.

Simmer the chicken breast fillets for 10 minutes, or until cooked.

Simmer the rice in the strained stock until tender.

Gently stir some of the hot soup into the egg mixture and beat thoroughly.

Add the shredded chicken breast fillets to the soup.

ADAS BIS SILQ
(Lentil and silverbeet soup)

Preparation time: 20 minutes
+ overnight refrigeration
Total cooking time:
3 hours 20 minutes
Serves 6

Chicken stock
1 kg (2 lb 4 oz) chicken trimmings
(necks, ribs, wings), fat removed
1 small onion, roughly chopped
1 bay leaf
3–4 sprigs fresh flat-leaf (Italian) parsley
1–2 sprigs fresh oregano or thyme

280 g (1½ cups) brown lentils, washed
850 g (1 lb 14 oz) silverbeet (Swiss
chard)
60 ml (¼ cup) olive oil
1 large onion, finely chopped
4 garlic cloves, crushed
25 g (½ cup) finely chopped fresh
coriander (cilantro) leaves
80 ml (⅓ cup) lemon juice
lemon wedges, to serve

1 To make the stock, place all the ingredients in a large saucepan, add 3 litres (12 cups) water and bring to the boil. Skim scum from the surface. Reduce the heat, simmer for 2 hours. Strain the stock, discarding the trimmings, onion and herbs. Chill overnight. You need 1 litre (4 cups).
2 Skim any fat from the stock. Place the lentils in a large saucepan, add the stock and 1 litre (4 cups) water. Bring to the boil, then reduce the heat and simmer, covered, for 1 hour.
3 Meanwhile, remove the stems from the silverbeet and shred the leaves. Heat the oil in a saucepan over medium heat and cook the onion for 2–3 minutes, or until transparent. Add the garlic and cook for 1 minute. Add the silverbeet and toss for 2–3 minutes, or until wilted. Stir into the lentils. Add the coriander and lemon juice, season, simmer, covered, for 15–20 minutes. Serve with the lemon wedges.

NUTRITION PER SERVE
Protein 52 g; Fat 15 g; Carbohydrate 20 g; Dietary Fibre 11 g; Cholesterol 83 mg; 1782 kJ (425 Cal)

Skim any fat from the surface of the stock before adding the lentils.

Stir the silverbeet into the onion mixture and cook until wilted.

Add the coriander and lemon juice to the silverbeet and lentil mixture.

CABBAGE ROLLS

Preparation time: 30 minutes
Total cooking time:
  1 hour 35 minutes
Makes 12 large rolls

1 tablespoon olive oil
1 onion, finely chopped
large pinch allspice
1 teaspoon ground cumin
large pinch ground nutmeg
2 bay leaves
1 large head of cabbage
500 g (1 lb 2 oz) minced (ground)
  lamb
220 g (1 cup) short-grain white rice
4 garlic cloves, crushed
50 g (1/3 cup) pine nuts toasted
2 tablespoons finely chopped fresh
  mint
2 tablespoons finely chopped fresh
  flat-leaf (Italian) parsley
1 tablespoon finely chopped raisins
250 ml (1 cup) olive oil, extra
80 ml (1/3 cup) lemon juice
extra virgin olive oil, to drizzle
lemon wedges, to serve

1 Heat the oil in a saucepan, add the onion and cook over medium heat for 10 minutes, or until golden. Add the allspice, cumin and nutmeg, and cook for 2 minutes, or until fragrant. Remove from the pan.
2 Bring a very large saucepan of water to the boil and add the bay leaves. Remove the tough outer leaves and about 5 cm (2 inch) of the core from the cabbage with a sharp knife, then place the cabbage into the boiling water. Cook for 5 minutes, then carefully loosen a whole leaf with tongs and remove. Continue to cook and remove the leaves until you reach the core. Drain, reserving the cooking liquid and set aside to cool.
3 Take 12 equal-size leaves and cut a small 'v' from the core end of each leaf to remove the thickest part, then trim the firm central veins so that the leaf is as flat as possible. Place three quarters of the remaining leaves into a very large saucepan to prevent the rolls catching on the base.
4 Combine the meat, onion mixture, rice, garlic, pine nuts, mint, parsley and raisins. Season. With the core

end of the leaf closest to you, form 2 tablespoons of the meat mixture into an oval and place in the centre of the leaf. Roll up, tucking in the sides to enclose the filling. Repeat with the other 11 leaves and filling. Place the rolls tightly in a single layer in the lined saucepan, seam-side down.
5 Combine 625 ml (2 1/2 cups) of the cooking liquid with the extra olive oil, lemon juice and 1 teaspoon salt, and pour over the rolls (the liquid

should just come to the top of the rolls). Lay the remaining leaves on top. Cover and bring to the boil, then reduce the heat and simmer for 1 hour 15 minutes, or until the filling is cooked. Remove with a slotted spoon and drizzle with extra virgin olive oil. Serve with lemon wedges.

NUTRITION PER ROLL
Protein 13 g; Fat 26 g; Carbohydrate 20 g;
Dietary Fibre 4 g; Cholesterol 28 mg;
1510 kJ (360 Cal)

Cook the cabbage in boiling water and remove the outer leaves as they cook.

Roll up the cabbage leaf, tucking in the sides, to enclose the filling.

TURKISH LAMB AND RICE PILAU

Preparation time: 20 minutes
  + 1 hour standing
Total cooking time: 35 minutes
Serves 4–6

1 large eggplant (aubergine) (500 g/
  1 lb 2 oz), cut into 1 cm (1/2 inch)
  cubes
125 ml (1/2 cup) olive oil
1 large onion, finely chopped
1 teaspoon ground cinnamon
2 teaspoons ground cumin
1 teaspoon ground coriander
300 g (101/2 oz) long-grain rice
500 ml (2 cups) chicken stock
500 g (1 lb 2 oz) minced (ground) lamb
1/2 teaspoon allspice
2 tablespoons olive oil, extra
2 tomatoes, cut into wedges
3 tablespoons pistachios toasted
2 tablespoons currants
2 tablespoons chopped fresh
  coriander (cilantro) leaves

1 Place the eggplant in a colander, sprinkle generously with salt and leave to stand for 1 hour. Rinse well and squeeze dry in a tea towel. Heat 2 tablespoons oil in a large, deep frying pan with a lid, and cook the eggplant over medium heat for 5–8 minutes, or until golden and cooked. Drain.
2 Heat the remaining oil in the pan and cook the onion for 2–3 minutes, or until soft but not brown. Stir in 1/2 teaspoon cinnamon, 1 teaspoon cumin and 1/2 teaspoon ground coriander. Stir in the rice, then add the stock, season and bring to the boil. Reduce the heat and simmer, covered, for 15 minutes, adding more water if the pilau starts to dry out.
3 Meanwhile, place the meat in a bowl with the allspice and remaining cumin, cinnamon and coriander. Season and mix together well. Roll into walnut-size balls. Heat the extra oil in the frying pan, add the meatballs in batches and cook over medium heat for 5 minutes, or until lightly browned and cooked through. Remove and drain on paper towels. Add the tomato to the pan and cook for 3–5 minutes or until turning lightly golden. Remove.
4 Stir the eggplant, pistachios, currants and meatballs through the rice (this should be quite dry). Spoon onto plates, place the cooked tomato around the edges and garnish with the coriander leaves.

NUTRITION PER SERVE (6)
Protein 25 g; Fat 40 g; Carbohydrate 45 g; Dietary Fibre 5 g; Cholesterol 55 mg; 2609 kJ (623 Cal)

Add the stock to the pan and bring to the boil.

Roll the lamb mixture into walnut-size balls.

Stir the eggplant, pistachios, currants and meatballs through the rice.

PASTICCIO
(Meat and pasta bake)

Preparation time: 25 minutes
+ 15 minutes resting
Total cooking time: 2 hours
Serves 4–6

60 ml (¼ cup) olive oil
1 onion, finely chopped
2 garlic cloves, crushed
80 g (2¾ oz) pancetta, finely chopped
500 g (1 lb 2 oz) minced (ground) beef
1 teaspoon chopped fresh oregano
60 g (2¼ oz) small button
  mushrooms, sliced
115 g (4 oz) chicken livers, trimmed
  and finely chopped
¼ teaspoon ground nutmeg
pinch cayenne pepper
60 ml (¼ cup) dry white wine
2 tablespoons tomato paste (purée)
375 ml (1½ cups) beef stock
2 tablespoons grated Parmesan cheese
1 egg, beaten
150 g (5 oz) macaroni
100 g (3½ oz) ricotta cheese
2 tablespoons milk
pinch cayenne pepper, extra
pinch ground nutmeg, extra
1 egg, beaten, extra
100 g (1 cup) grated Parmesan
  cheese, extra

Béchamel sauce
40 g (1½ oz) butter
1½ tablespoons plain (alll-purpose)
  flour
pinch ground nutmeg
300 ml (10½ fl oz) milk
1 small bay leaf

1 Preheat the oven to 180°C (350°F/ Gas 4). Grease a 1.5 litre (6 cup) ovenproof dish. Heat the oil in a large frying pan over medium heat and cook the onion, garlic and pancetta, stirring, for 5–6 minutes, or until the onion is golden. Add the beef, increase the heat and stir for 5 minutes, or until browned.

2 Add the oregano, mushrooms, chicken livers, nutmeg and cayenne, season and cook for 2 minutes, or until the livers change colour. Add the wine and cook over high heat for 1 minute, or until evaporated. Stir in the tomato paste and stock. Reduce the heat and simmer for 45 minutes, or until thickened. Beat the Parmesan and egg together, and quickly stir through the sauce.

3 Cook the macaroni in lightly salted boiling water until *al dente*. Meanwhile, blend the ricotta, milk, extra cayenne, extra nutmeg, extra egg and 25 g (¼ cup) extra Parmesan. Season. Drain the macaroni, add to the ricotta mixture and mix well.

4 To make the béchamel sauce, melt the butter in a small saucepan. Stir in the flour and cook over low heat until just golden; stir in the nutmeg. Take off the heat and gradually stir in the milk. Add the bay leaf. Season. Return to low heat and simmer, stirring, until thickened. Discard the bay leaf.

5 Spread half the meat sauce in the dish, top with half the pasta and half the remaining Parmesan. Layer with the remaining meat sauce and pasta; press down with the back of a spoon. Spread the béchamel on top, then top with remaining Parmesan. Bake for 45–50 minutes, or until golden. Rest for 15 minutes before serving.

NUTRITION PER SERVE (6)
Protein 43 g; Fat 40 g; Carbohydrate 27 g; Dietary Fibre 2.5 g; Cholesterol 192 mg; 2670 kJ (638 Cal)

Cook the mixture for 2 minutes, or until the chicken livers change colour.

Add the tomato paste and stock, then simmer until thickened.

Stir the cooked, drained macaroni through the ricotta mixture.

Gradually add the milk to the butter and flour to make the béchamel sauce.

Spoon half the pasta and ricotta mixture over the meat sauce.

Pour the béchamel sauce evenly over the top pasta layer.

PASTA E FAGIOLI
(Pasta and bean soup)

Preparation time: 15 minutes
  + overnight soaking
  + 10 minutes resting
Total cooking time:
  1 hour 45 minutes
Serves 4

200 g (7 oz) dried borlotti beans
60 ml (¼ cup) olive oil
90 g (3¼ oz) piece pancetta, finely
  diced
1 onion, finely chopped
2 garlic cloves, crushed
1 celery stick, thinly sliced
1 carrot, diced
1 bay leaf
1 sprig fresh rosemary
1 sprig fresh flat-leaf (Italian) parsley
400 g (14 oz) can diced tomatoes,
  drained
1.5 litres (6½ cups) vegetable stock
2 tablespoons finely chopped fresh
  flat-leaf (Italian) parsley
150 g (5½ oz) ditalini or other small
  dried pasta
extra virgin olive oil, to drizzle
freshly grated Parmesan cheese,
  to serve

1 Place the beans in a large bowl, cover with cold water and leave to soak overnight. Drain and rinse.
2 Heat the oil in a large saucepan, add the pancetta, onion, garlic, celery and carrot, and cook over medium heat for 5 minutes, or until golden. Season with pepper. Add the bay leaf, rosemary, parsley, tomato, stock and beans, and bring to the boil. Reduce the heat and simmer for 1½ hours, or until the beans are tender. Add more boiling water if necessary to maintain the liquid level.
3 Discard the bay leaf, rosemary and parsley sprigs. Scoop out 1 cup of the bean mixture and purée in a food processor or blender. Return to the pan, season with salt and ground black pepper, and add the parsley and pasta. Simmer for 6 minutes, or until the pasta is *al dente*. Remove from the heat and set aside for 10 minutes. Serve drizzled with extra virgin olive oil and garnished with Parmesan.

NUTRITION PER SERVE
Protein 13 g; Fat 20 g; Carbohydrate 38 g; Dietary Fibre 7.5 g; Cholesterol 12 mg; 1643 kJ (393 Cal)

Cook the pancetta, onion, garlic, celery and carrot for 5 minutes.

Purée 1 cup of the bean mixture in a food processor.

Add the pasta to the soup and cook until al dente.

OSSO BUCCO DI GREMOLATA
(Italian veal shank stew)

Preparation time: 30 minutes
Total cooking time:
  2 hours 20 minutes
Serves 4–6

12 meaty pieces veal shank,
  osso bucco style
40 g (1/3 cup) plain (all-purpose) flour,
  seasoned
20 g (1/2 oz) butter
80 ml (1/3 cup) olive oil
1 onion, diced
1 carrot, diced
1 celery stick, diced
1 bay leaf
1 garlic clove, crushed
500 ml (2 cups) veal or chicken stock
250 ml (1 cup) white wine
80 ml (1/3 cup) lemon juice

Gremolata
12 g (2/3 cup) fresh flat-leaf (Italian)
  parsley, finely chopped
2 garlic cloves, finely chopped
1 tablespoon grated lemon zest

1 Lightly dust the veal shanks in the seasoned flour. Heat the butter and 60 ml (1/4 cup) oil in a large deep-sided frying pan over high heat until sizzling. Add the veal and cook in batches for 5 minutes, or until brown all over. Remove from the pan.
2 Heat the remaining oil in a large saucepan and add the onion, carrot, celery and bay leaf, and cook for 10 minutes, or until softened and starting to brown. Stir in the garlic, stock, wine and lemon juice, scraping the bottom of the pan to remove any sediment. Add the veal, bring to the boil then reduce the heat to low, cover and simmer for 1 1/2–2 hours, or until the veal is very tender and falling off the bone and the sauce has reduced. Season to taste.
3 To make the gremolata, combine the parsley, garlic and rind. Sprinkle over the osso bucco just before serving. Serve with soft polenta.

NUTRITION PER SERVE (6)
Protein 53 g; Fat 17 g; Carbohydrate 7.5 g; Dietary Fibre 1.5 g; Cholesterol 205 mg; 1759 kJ (420 Cal)

Cook the veal shank pieces in batches until well browned.

Cook the onion, carrot, celery and bay leaf until softened.

Simmer until the veal is very tender and the sauce has reduced.

LAMB TAGINE

Preparation time: 15 minutes
+ 1 hour marinating
Total cooking time:
1 hour 45 minutes
Serves 6–8

1.5 kg (3 lb 5 oz) leg or shoulder
lamb, cut into 2.5 cm (1 inch) pieces
3 garlic cloves, chopped
80 ml (1/3 cup) olive oil
2 teaspoons ground cumin
1 teaspoon ground ginger
1 teaspoon ground turmeric
1 teaspoon paprika
1/2 teaspoon ground cinnamon
2 onions, thinly sliced
600 ml (21 fl oz) beef stock
1/4 preserved lemon, pulp discarded,
rind rinsed and cut into thin strips
425 g (15 oz) can chickpeas, drained
35 g (1 1/4 oz) cracked green olives
3 tablespoons chopped fresh
coriander (cilantro) leaves

1 Place the lamb in a non-metallic bowl, add the garlic, 2 tablespoons olive oil and the ground cumin, ginger, turmeric, paprika, cinnamon, and 1/2 teaspoon ground black pepper and 1 teaspoon salt. Mix well to coat and leave to marinate for 1 hour.
2 Heat the remaining oil in a large saucepan, add the lamb in batches and cook over high heat for 2–3 minutes, or until browned. Remove from the pan. Add the onion and cook for 2 minutes, return the meat to the pan and add the beef stock. Reduce the heat and simmer, covered, for 1 hour. Add the preserved lemon, chickpeas and olives, and cook, uncovered, for a further 30 minutes, or until the meat is tender and the sauce reduced and thickened. Stir in the coriander. Serve in bowls with couscous.

NUTRITION PER SERVE (8)
Protein 50 g; Fat 20 g; Carbohydrate 11 g; Dietary Fibre 5.5 g; Cholesterol 124 mg; 1765 kJ (422 Cal)

COOK'S FILE
Note: If you prefer, you can bake this lamb in the oven in a covered casserole dish. Preheat the oven to 190°C (375°F/ Gas 5) and cook the tagine for about 1 hour, adding the lemon, chickpeas and olives after 40 minutes.

Coat the lamb in the spice marinade, then leave for 1 hour.

Cook the lamb in batches over high heat until browned.

Add the preserved lemon, chickpeas and cracked green olives to the pan.

KEFTA GHAN' MI BEL'
(Lamb kefta)

Preparation time: 30 minutes
Total cooking time: 40 minutes
Serves 4

1 kg (2 lb 4 oz) minced (ground) lamb
1 onion, finely chopped
2 garlic cloves, finely chopped
2 tablespoons finely chopped fresh
    flat-leaf (Italian) parsley
2 tablespoons finely chopped fresh
    coriander (cilantro) leaves
1/2 teaspoon cayenne pepper
1/2 teaspoon ground allspice
1/2 teaspoon ground ginger
1/2 teaspoon ground cardamom
1 teaspoon ground cumin
1 teaspoon paprika

Sauce
2 tablespoons olive oil
1 onion, finely chopped
2 garlic cloves, finely chopped
2 teaspoons ground cumin
1/2 teaspoon ground cinnamon
1 teaspoon paprika
2 x 425 g (15 oz) cans chopped
    tomatoes
2 teaspoons harissa
4 tablespoons chopped fresh
    coriander (coriander) leaves

1 Preheat the oven to 180°C (350°F/ Gas 4). Lightly grease two baking trays. Place the lamb, onion, garlic, herbs and spices in a bowl and mix together well. Season to taste. Roll tablespoons of the mixture into balls and place on the prepared trays. Bake for 18–20 minutes, or until browned.
2 Meanwhile, to make the sauce, heat the oil in a large saucepan, add the onion and cook over medium heat for 5 minutes, or until soft. Add the garlic, cumin, cinnamon and paprika, and cook for 1 minute, or until fragrant.
3 Stir in the tomato and harissa, and bring to the boil. Reduce the heat and simmer for 20 minutes, then add the meatballs and simmer for 10 minutes, or until cooked through. Stir in the coriander, season well and serve.

NUTRITION PER SERVE
Protein 53 g; Fat 37 g; Carbohydrate 10 g; Dietary Fibre 4 g; Cholesterol 158 mg; 2434 kJ (580 Cal)

Roll tablespoons of the lamb mixture into balls.

Add the spices to the onion and cook until fragrant.

Simmer the meatballs in the tomato sauce until cooked through.

KIBBEH BIL SANIEH
(Layered lamb and burghul)

Preparation time: 30 minutes
+ 30 minutes soaking
+ 10 minutes cooling
Total cooking time: 50 minutes
Serves 4–6

350 g (2 cups) burghul (bulgar)
400 g (14 oz) minced (ground) lamb
1 large onion, finely chopped
1 tablespoon ground cumin
1 teaspoon allspice
olive oil, for brushing

Filling
1 tablespoon olive oil, plus extra
   for brushing
1 onion, finely chopped
1 teaspoon ground cinnamon
1 tablespoon ground cumin
500 g (1 lb 2 oz) minced (ground) lamb
80 g (1/2 cup) raisins
100 g (3 1/2 oz) pine nuts, toasted

1 Soak the burghul in cold water for 30 minutes, drain and squeeze out excess water. Place the lamb, onion, cumin, allspice, salt and pepper in a food processor, and process until combined. Add the burghul and process to a paste. Refrigerate until needed. Preheat the oven to 180°C (350°F/Gas 4). Grease a 20 cm x 30 cm (8 inch x 12 inch) roasting tin.

2 To make the filling, heat the oil in a large frying pan over medium heat and cook the onion for 5 minutes, or until softened. Add the cinnamon and cumin, and stir for 1 minute, or until fragrant. Add the lamb, stirring to break up any lumps, and cook for 5 minutes, or until the meat is brown.

Stir in the raisins and nuts and season.

3 Press half the burghul mixture into the base of the tin, smoothing the surface with wetted hands. Spread the filling over the top, then cover with the remaining burghul, again smoothing the surface.

4 Score a diamond pattern in the top of the mixture with a sharp knife and brush lightly with olive oil. Bake for 35–40 minutes, or until the top is brown and crisp. Cool for 10 minutes before cutting into diamond shapes. Serve with yoghurt and salad.

NUTRITION PER SERVE (6)
Protein 40 g; Fat 25 g; Carbohydrate 50 g; Dietary Fibre 3.5 g; Cholesterol 100 mg; 2448 kJ (585 Cal)

Process the meat mixture and the burghul to a paste.

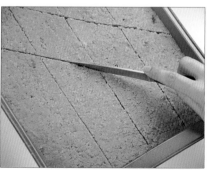

Spread the mea filling over the burghul layer.

Using a sharp knife, score a diamond pattern into the top.

SOUVLAKE
(Skewered lamb)

Preparation time: 20 minutes
  + overnight marinating
  + 30 minutes standing
Total cooking time: 10 minutes
Serves 4

1 kg (2 lb 4 oz) boned leg lamb,
  trimmed, cut into 2 cm (inch) cubes
60 ml (¼ cup) olive oil
2 teaspoons finely grated lemon rind
80 ml (⅓ cup) lemon juice
2 teaspoons dried oregano

125 ml (½ cup) dry white wine
2 large garlic cloves, finely chopped
2 fresh bay leaves
250 g (1 cup) Greek-style plain
  yoghurt
2 garlic cloves, crushed, extra

1 Place the lamb in a non-metallic
bowl with 2 tablespoons of the olive
oil, the lemon rind and juice,
oregano, wine, garlic and bay leaves.
Season with black pepper and toss to
coat. Cover and refrigerate overnight.
2 Place the yoghurt and extra garlic
in a bowl, mix together well and
leave for 30 minutes.
3 Drain the lamb and pat dry. Thread

onto 8 skewers and cook on a
barbecue or chargrill plate (griddle),
brushing with the remaining oil,
for 7–8 minutes, or until brown
on the outside and still a little rare
in the middle. Drizzle with the
garlic yoghurt and serve with
warm pitta bread and a salad.

NUTRITION PER SERVE
Protein 43 g; Fat 20 g; Carbohydrate 4 g;
Dietary Fibre 0 g; Cholesterol 126 mg;
1660 kJ (397 Cal)

COOK'S FILE
Note: If using wooden skewers, soak
them in water for 30 minutes to prevent
burning during cooking.

Toss the lamb to coat well with the spicy marinade.

Pat the drained lamb dry and thread onto eight skewers.

Brush the remaining oil over the lamb skewers during cooking.

MINESTRONE WITH PESTO
(Italian vegetable soup
with basil sauce)

Preparation time: 25 minutes
+ overnight soaking
Total cooking time: 2 hours
Serves 6

125 g (4¹/2 oz) dried borlotti beans
1 large onion, coarsely chopped
2 garlic cloves
3 tablespoons coarsely chopped
    fresh flat-leaf (Italian) parsley
60 g (2¹/4 oz) pancetta, chopped
3 tablespoons olive oil
1 celery stick, halved lengthways,
    then cut into 1 cm (¹/2 inch) slices
1 carrot, halved lengthways, then
    cut into 1 cm (¹/2 inch) slices
1 potato, diced
2 teaspoons tomato paste (purée)
400 g (14 oz) can Italian diced
    tomatoes
6 fresh basil leaves, roughly torn
2 litres (8 cups) chicken or vegetable
    stock
2 thin zucchini (courgettes), cut into
    1.5 cm (⁵/8 inch) slices
115 g (³/4 cup) shelled peas
60 g (2¹/4 oz) green beans, cut into
    4 cm (1¹/2 inch) lengths
80 g (2³/4 oz) silverbeet (Swiss chard)
    leaves, shredded
75 g (2¹/2 oz) ditalini or other small
    pasta

Pesto
30 g (1 cup) fresh basil leaves
20 g (¹/2 oz) pine nuts lightly toasted
2 garlic cloves
100 ml (3¹/2 fl oz) olive oil
25 g (¹/4 cup) freshly grated Parmesan
    cheese

1 Put the beans in a large bowl, cover with water and soak overnight. Drain and rinse under cold water.
2 Process the onion, garlic, parsley and pancetta in a food processor until fine. Heat the oil in a saucepan and cook the pancetta mix over low heat, stirring occasionally, for 8–10 minutes.
3 Add the celery, carrot and potato, and cook for 5 minutes, then stir in the tomato paste, tomato, basil and borlotti beans. Season. Add the stock and bring to the boil. Cover and simmer, stirring occasionally, for 1 hour 30 minutes.

4 Season and add the zucchini, peas, green beans, silverbeet and pasta. Simmer for 8–10 minutes, or until the vegetables and pasta are *al dente*.
5 To make the pesto, process the basil, pine nuts and garlic with a pinch of salt in a food processor until finely chopped. With the motor running, slowly add the oil. Transfer to a bowl and stir in the Parmesan and pepper. Serve the soup with pesto on top.

NUTRITION PER SERVE
Protein 9 g; Fat 30 g; Carbohydrate 20 g;
Dietary Fibre 5.3 g; Cholesterol 9 mg;
1593 kJ (380 Cal)

Cook the processed onion, garlic, parsley and pancetta mixture.

Simmer until the pasta and vegetables are al dente.

Stir the Parmesan into the finely chopped basil mixture.

MOUSSAKA
(Lamb and eggplant bake)

Preparation time: 20 minutes
 + 40 minutes standing
Total cooking time:
 1 hour 50 minutes
Serves 6

2 large ripe tomatoes
1.5 kg (3 lb 5 oz) eggplant (aubergines),
 cut into 5 mm (¼ inch) slices
125 ml (½ cup) light olive oil
1 tablespoon olive oil
2 onions, finely chopped
2 large garlic cloves, crushed
½ teaspoon ground allspice
1¼ teaspoons ground cinnamon
750 g (1 lb 10 oz) minced (ground)
 lamb
2 tablespoons tomato paste (purée)
125 ml (½ cup) white wine
3 tablespoons chopped fresh
 flat-leaf (Italian) parsley

White sauce
50 g (1¾ oz) butter
60 g (½ cup) plain (all-purpose) flour
600 ml (21 fl oz) milk
pinch ground nutmeg
35 g (⅓ cup) finely grated kefalotyri
 or Parmesan cheese
2 eggs, lightly beaten

1 Preheat the oven to 180°C (350°F/ Gas 4). Score a cross in the base of each tomato. Place in a bowl of boiling water for 1 minute, then plunge into cold water. Peel the skin away from the cross. Roughly chop. Lay the eggplant on a tray, sprinkle with salt and leave to stand for 30 minutes. Rinse and pat dry.
2 Heat 2 tablespoons olive oil in a frying pan, and cook the eggplant in 4–5 batches for 1–2 minutes each side, or until golden and soft. Add more oil when needed.
3 Heat the oil in a saucepan and cook the onion over medium heat for 5 minutes. Add the garlic, allspice and cinnamon and cook for 30 seconds. Add the meat and cook for 5 minutes, or until browned, breaking up any lumps. Add the tomato, tomato paste and wine, and simmer over low heat for 30 minutes, or until the liquid has evaporated. Stir in parsley and season.

4 Meanwhile, to make the white sauce, melt the butter in a saucepan over medium heat. Add the flour and cook for 1 minute. Remove from the heat and gradually stir in the milk and nutmeg. Return to the heat and simmer for 2 minutes. Add 1 tablespoon of the cheese and stir well. Stir in the egg just before using.
5 Line the base of a 3 litre (12 cup) 25 cm x 30 cm (10 inch x 12 inch)

Cook the tomato and mince mixture until the liquid has evaporated.

ovenproof dish with a third of the eggplant. Spoon on half the meat and cover with a second layer of eggplant. Top with remaining meat and eggplant. Pour on the white sauce and sprinkle with remaining cheese. Bake for 1 hour. Leave for 10 minutes before slicing.

NUTRITION PER SERVE
Protein 34 g; Fat 47 g; Carbohydrate 15 g;
Dietary Fibre 7 g; Cholesterol 173 mg;
2609 kJ (623 Cal)

Pour the white sauce over the final layer of eggplant.

93

Coat the pork fillet pieces in the ground coriander and pepper.

Heat some oil in a frying pan and cook the pork in batches until brown.

Remove the meat from the pan and keep warm.

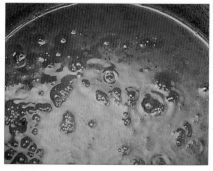

Boil the liquid until reduced and slightly thickened.

AFELIA
(Cypriot pork and coriander stew)

Preparation time: 15 minutes
+ overnight marinating
Total cooking time:
1 hour 20 minutes
Serves 4–6

1½ tablespoons coriander seeds
800 g (1 lb 12 oz) pork fillet, cut into
2 cm (¾ inch) dice
1 tablespoon plain (all-purpose) flour
60 ml (¼ cup) olive oil
1 large onion, thinly sliced
375 ml (1½ cups) red wine
250 ml (1 cup) chicken stock
1 teaspoon sugar
fresh coriander (cilantro) sprigs, to
garnish

1 Crush the coriander seeds in a mortar and pestle. Combine the pork, crushed seeds and ½ teaspoon cracked pepper in a bowl. Cover and marinate overnight in the fridge.
2 Combine the flour and pork and toss. Heat 2 tablespoons oil in a frying pan and cook the pork in batches over high heat for 1–2 minutes, or until brown. Remove.
3 Heat the remaining oil, add the onion and cook over medium heat for 2–3 minutes, or until just golden. Return the meat to the pan, add the red wine, stock and sugar, and season. Bring to the boil, then reduce the heat and simmer, covered, for 1 hour.
4 Remove the meat. Return the pan to the heat and boil over high heat for 3–5 minutes, or until reduced and slightly thickened. Pour over the meat and top with the coriander.

NUTRITION PER SERVE (6)
Protein 30 g; Fat 12 g; Carbohydrate 2.5 g;
Dietary Fibre 0 g; Cholesterol 65 mg;
1180 kJ (282 Cal)

Using a small, sharp knife, remove the chokes from the artichokes.

Fill each artichoke with some of the lamb mixture.

AROISHAWKI MIHSHI
(Middle eastern stuffed artichokes)

Preparation time:
  1 hour 30 minutes
Total cooking time:
  1 hour 25 minutes
Serves 6

140 ml (4¹/² fl oz) lemon juice
12 globe artichokes
500 g (1 lb 2 oz) minced (ground) lamb
40 g (¹/² cup) fresh breadcrumbs
1 egg, lightly beaten
1 tablespoon chopped fresh thyme
olive oil, for deep-frying
125 ml (¹/² cup) extra virgin olive oil
375 ml (1¹/² cups) chicken stock
¹/² teaspoon ground turmeric
1 bay leaf
40 g (1¹/² oz) butter
2 tablespoons plain (all-purpose) flour

1 Fill a large bowl with water and add 60 ml (¹/₄ cup) lemon juice. Peel the outer leaves from the artichokes, trimming the base and stem to reveal the bottom. Cut the tops off to reveal the chokes and remove. Place all the artichokes in the bowl of lemon water.
2 Place the lamb, breadcrumbs, egg and thyme in a bowl, season and mix well. Pat the artichokes dry with paper towels. Fill each artichoke with 2 tablespoons of the lamb mixture.
3 Fill a large heavy-based saucepan one-third full of oil and heat to 180°C (350°F), or until a cube of bread browns in 15 seconds. Cook the artichokes in batches for 5 minutes, or until golden brown. Drain.
4 Place the extra virgin olive oil, 250 ml (1 cup) stock, turmeric, bay leaf and remaining lemon juice in a 1.25 litre (5 cup) casserole dish. Season. Bring to the boil, add the artichokes and simmer, covered, for 1 hour, or until tender, adding more stock if needed. Turn the artichokes twice during cooking. Remove the artichokes and keep warm. Reserve the liquid.
5 Melt the butter in a saucepan, add the flour and stir for 1 minute, or until pale and foamy. Remove from the heat and gradually stir in the reserved liquid. Return to the heat and stir until the sauce boils and thickens, then reduce the heat and simmer for 2 minutes. Serve immediately with the artichokes.

Deep-fry the stuffed artichokes until golden brown.

Remove the artichokes from the cooking liquid with a slotted spoon.

NUTRITION PER SERVE
Protein 30 g; Fat 37 g; Carbohydrate 4.5 g; Dietary Fibre 0 g; Cholesterol 82 mg; 1968 kJ (470 Cal)

CHICKEN AND PORK PAELLA

Preparation time: 30 minutes
Total cooking time: 1 hour
Serves 6

60 ml (¼ cup) olive oil
1 large red capsicum (pepper), seeded
   and cut into 5 mm (¼ inch) strips
600 g (1 lb 5 oz) chicken thigh fillets,
   cut into 3 cm (1¼ inch) cubes
200 g (7 oz) chorizo sausage, cut into
   2 cm (¾ inch) slices
200 g (7 oz) mushrooms, thinly sliced
3 garlic cloves, crushed
1 tablespoon lemon zest
700 g (1 lb 9 oz) tomatoes, roughly
   chopped
200 g (7 oz) green beans, cut into
   3 cm (1¼ inch) lengths
1 tablespoon chopped fresh rosemary
2 tablespoons chopped fresh flat-leaf
   (Italian) parsley
¼ teaspoon saffron threads dissolved
   in 60 ml (¼ cup) hot water
440 g (2 cups) short-grain rice
750 ml (3 cups) hot chicken stock
6 lemon wedges

1 Heat the oil in a large, deep frying or paella pan over medium heat. Add the capsicum and cook for 6 minutes, or until softened. Remove from pan.
2 Add the chicken to the pan and cook for 10 minutes, or until brown on all sides. Remove. Add the sausage to the pan and cook for 5 minutes, or until golden on all sides. Remove.
3 Add the mushrooms, garlic and lemon zest, and cook over medium heat for 5 minutes. Stir in the tomato and capsicum, and cook for a further 5 minutes, or until the tomato is soft.

4 Add the beans, rosemary, parsley, saffron mixture, rice, chicken and sausage. Stir briefly and add the stock. Do not stir at this point. Reduce the heat and simmer for 30 minutes. Remove from the heat, cover and leave to stand for 10 minutes. Serve with lemon wedges.

NUTRITION PER SERVE
Protein 34 g; Fat 20 g; Carbohydrate 63 g;
Dietary Fibre 5 g; Cholesterol 72 mg;
2388 kJ (571 Cal)

COOK'S FILE
Note: Paellas are not stirred right to the bottom of the pan during cooking in the hope that a thin crust of crispy rice will form. This is considered one of the best parts of the paella. For this reason, it is important not to use a non-stick frying pan. Paellas are traditionally served at the table from the pan.
Variation: Try adding shellfish such as prawns (shrimp) 5–10 minutes after adding the stock.

Cut the chorizo sausage into 2 cm (³/4 inch) thick slices.

Add the tomato and capsicum and cook until the tomato is soft.

Pour the chicken stock into the pan and do not stir.

CHICKEN WITH PRESERVED LEMON AND OLIVES

Preparation time: 10 minutes
Total cooking time: 1 hour
Serves 4

60 ml (¼ cup) olive oil
1.6 kg (3 lb 8 oz) free-range chicken
1 onion, chopped
2 garlic cloves, chopped
600 ml (21 fl oz) chicken stock
½ teaspoon ground ginger
1½ teaspoons ground cinnamon
pinch saffron threads
100 g (3½ oz) green olives
¼ preserved lemon, pulp removed,
    rind washed and cut into slivers
2 bay leaves
2 chicken livers
3 tablespoons chopped fresh
    coriander (cilantro) leaves

1 Preheat the oven to 180°C (350°F/ Gas 4). Heat 2 tablespoons oil in a large frying pan, add the chicken and brown on all sides. Place in a deep baking dish.
2 Heat the remaining oil, add the onion and garlic and cook over medium heat for 3–4 minutes, or until softened. Add the stock, ginger, cinnamon, saffron, olives, lemon and bay leaves and pour around the chicken. Bake for 45 minutes, adding a little more water or stock if the sauce gets too dry.
3 Remove the chicken from the dish, cover with foil and leave to rest. Discard the bay leaves. Pour the contents of the baking dish into a frying pan, add the chicken livers and mash into the sauce as they cook.

Cook for 5–6 minutes, or until the sauce has reduced and thickened. Add the coriander. Cut the chicken into four and serve with the sauce.

NUTRITION PER SERVE
Protein 85 g; Fat 30 g; Carbohydrate 5 g; Dietary Fibre 1.5 g; Cholesterol 576 mg; 2610 kJ (624 Cal)

Pour the chicken stock mixture around the chicken.

Bake the chicken for 45 minutes, adding stock or water if it is too dry.

Mash the chicken livers into the sauce so they thicken it as they cook.

SWEET FINISHES

PEACHES POACHED IN WINE

Preparation time: 20 minutes
Total cooking time: 20 minutes
Serves 4

4 just-ripe yellow-fleshed freestone
    peaches
500 ml (2 cups) sweet white wine
    such as Sauternes
60 ml (¼ cup) orange liqueur
250 g (1 cup) sugar
1 cinnamon stick
1 vanilla bean, split
8 fresh mint leaves
mascarpone or crème fraîche,
    to serve

1 Cut a small cross in the base of each peach. Immerse the peaches in boiling water for 30 seconds, then drain and cool slightly. Peel off the skin, cut in half and carefully remove the stones.
2 Place the wine, liqueur, sugar, cinnamon stick and vanilla bean in a deep-sided frying pan large enough to hold the peach halves in a single layer. Heat the mixture, stirring, until the sugar dissolves. Bring to the boil, then reduce the heat and simmer for 5 minutes. Add the peaches to the pan and simmer for 4 minutes, turning them over halfway through. Remove with a slotted spoon and leave to cool. Continue to simmer the syrup for 6–8 minutes, or until thick. Strain and set aside.
3 Arrange the peaches on a serving platter, cut-side-up. Spoon the syrup over the top and garnish each half with a mint leaf. Serve the peaches warm or chilled, with a dollop of mascarpone or crème fraîche.

NUTRITION PER SERVE
Protein 3 g; Fat 6.5 g; Carbohydrate 74 g;
Dietary Fibre 2 g; Cholesterol 19 mg;
1900 kJ (455 Cal)

COOK'S FILE
Note: There are two types of peach, the freestone and the clingstone. As the names imply, clingstone indicates that the flesh will cling to the stone whereas the stones in freestone peaches are easily removed without breaking up the flesh. Each has a variety with either yellow or white flesh, and all these peaches are equally delicious.

Peel the skin away from the cross cut in the base of the peaches.

Simmer the wine, liqueur, sugar, cinnamon and vanilla bean.

CHERRY CLAFOUTIS
(French batter pudding)

Preparation time: 15 minutes
Total cooking time: 40 minutes
Serves 6–8

500 g (1 lb 2 oz) fresh cherries (see Hint)
90 g (¾ cup) plain (all-purpose) flour
2 eggs, lightly beaten
90 g (⅓ cup) caster (superfine) sugar
250 ml (1 cup) milk
60 ml (¼ cup) thick (double/heavy) cream

50 g (1¾ oz) unsalted butter, melted
icing (confectioner's) sugar, for dusting

1 Preheat the oven to 180°C (350°F/ Gas 4). Lightly brush a 1.5 litre (6 cup) ovenproof dish with melted butter.
2 Carefully pit the cherries, then spread into the dish in a single layer.
3 Sift the flour into a bowl, add the eggs and whisk until smooth. Add the sugar, milk, cream and butter, whisking until just combined, but being careful not to overbeat.
4 Pour the batter over the cherries and bake for 30–40 minutes, or until a skewer comes out clean when inserted into the centre. Remove from

the oven and dust generously with icing sugar. Serve immediately.

NUTRITION PER SERVE (8)
Protein 4.5 g; Fat 11 g; Carbohydrate 23 g; Dietary Fibre 1.5 g; Cholesterol 75 mg; 855 kJ (204 Cal)

COOK'S FILE
Hint: You can use a 720 g (1 lb 9½ oz) jar of cherries. Make sure you thoroughly drain the juice away.
Variation: Blueberries, blackberries, raspberries, or small, well-flavoured strawberries can be used. A delicious version can be made using slices of poached pear.

Add the sugar, milk, cream and butter to the flour mixture and whisk well.

Pour the batter over the single layer of cherries.

Cook until the batter is golden brown and nicely set.

FIGS IN HONEY SYRUP

Preparation time: 15 minutes
Total cooking time: 1 hour
Serves 4

100 g (3½ oz) blanched whole
    almonds
12–16 whole fresh figs (see Note)
125 g (½ cup) sugar
115 g (⅓ cup) honey
2 tablespoons lemon juice
6 cm (2½ inch) sliver of lemon rind
1 cinnamon stick
250 g (1 cup) plain Greek-style yoghurt

1 Preheat the oven to 180°C (350°F/ Gas 4). Place the almonds on a baking tray and bake for 5 minutes, or until golden brown. Cool. Cut the tops off the figs and make a small incision 5 mm (¼ inch) down the top of each one. Push an almond into the base of each fig. Roughly chop the remaining almonds.

2 Place 750 ml (3 cups) water in a saucepan; stir the sugar over medium heat until it dissolves. Increase the heat and bring to the boil. Stir in the honey, juice, rind and cinnamon. Reduce the heat to medium, gently place the figs in the pan and cook for 30 minutes. Transfer with a slotted spoon to a large serving dish.

3 Boil the liquid over high heat for 15–20 minutes, or until thick and syrupy. Remove the cinnamon and rind. Cool the syrup slightly and pour over the figs. Sprinkle with the remaining almonds. Serve warm or cold with yoghurt.

NUTRITION PER SERVE
Protein 11 g; Fat 17 g; Carbohydrate 74 g; Dietary Fibre 7 g; Cholesterol 10 mg; 2017 kJ (482 Cal)

COOK'S FILE
Note: You can also use 500 g (1 lb 2 oz) dried whole figs. Cover with 750 ml (3 cups) cold water and soak for 8 hours. Drain, reserving the liquid. Push a blanched almond into the bottom of each fig. Place the liquid in a large saucepan, add the sugar and bring to the boil, stirring as the sugar dissolves. Add the honey, lemon juice, lemon rind and cinnamon stick, and continue the recipe as above.

Make a small crossways incision in the top of each fig.

Push a blanched almond into the base of each fig.

Using a slotted spoon, remove the figs from the pan.

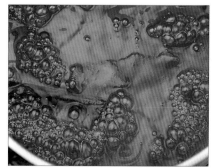

Continue to boil the liquid until thick and syrupy.

LEMON GRANITA

Preparation time: 15 minutes
  + 2 hours freezing
Total cooking time: 5 minutes
Serves 6

315 ml (1¼ cups) lemon juice
1 tablespoon lemon zest
200 g (7 oz) caster (superfine) sugar

1 Place the lemon juice, lemon zest and caster sugar in a small saucepan and stir over low heat for 5 minutes, or until the sugar is dissolved. Remove from the heat and leave to cool.
2 Add 500 ml (2 cups) water to the juice mixture and mix together well. Pour the mixture into a shallow 30 cm x 20 cm (12 inch x 8 inch) metal container and place in the freezer until the mixture is beginning to freeze around the edges. Scrape the frozen sections back into the mixture with a fork. Repeat every 30 minutes until the mixture has even-size ice crystals. Beat the mixture with a fork just before serving. To serve, spoon the lemon granita into six chilled glasses.

NUTRITION PER SERVE
Protein 0 g; Fat 0 g; Carbohydrate 35 g; Dietary Fibre 0 g; Cholesterol 0 mg; 592 kJ (140 Cal)

Stir the juice, zest and sugar over low heat until the sugar has dissolved.

Scrape the frozen edges of the mixture back into the centre.

Beat the granita mixture with a fork just prior to serving.

YOGHURT CAKE WITH SYRUP

Preparation time: 20 minutes
Total cooking time: 1 hour
Serves 8–10

185 g (6¼ oz) unsalted butter, softened
250 g (1 cup) caster (superfine) sugar
5 eggs, separated
250 g (1 cup) plain Greek-style yoghurt
2 teaspoons grated lemon zest
½ teaspoon vanilla essence
280 g (2¼ cups) plain (all-purpose) flour
2 teaspoons baking powder
½ teaspoon bicarbonate of soda
whipped cream, to serve

Syrup
250 g (1 cup) caster (superfine) sugar
1 cinnamon stick
4 cm (1½ inch) strip lemon rind
1 tablespoon lemon juice

1 Preheat the oven to 180°C (350°F/ Gas 4) and lightly grease a 20 cm x 10 cm (8 inch x 4 inch) loaf tin.
2 Place the butter and sugar in a bowl and beat until light and creamy. Add the egg yolks gradually, beating well after each addition. Stir in the yoghurt, lemon rind and vanilla essence. Fold in the sifted flour, baking powder and bicarbonate of soda with a metal spoon.
3 Whisk the egg whites in a clean, dry bowl until stiff, and fold into the mixture. Spoon into the prepared tin and bake for 50 minutes, or until a skewer comes out clean when inserted into the centre of the cake. Cool in the tin for 10 minutes, then turn out onto a wire rack to cool.

4 Meanwhile, to make the syrup, place the sugar and cinnamon stick in a small pan with 185 ml (¾ cup) cold water. Stir over medium heat until the sugar is dissolved. Bring to the boil, add the lemon rind and juice, then reduce the heat and simmer for 5–6 minutes. Strain.

5 Pour the syrup over the cake and wait for most of it to be absorbed before serving. Cut into slices and serve warm with whipped cream.

NUTRITION PER SERVE (10)
Protein 7.5 g; Fat 19 g; Carbohydrate 72 g; Dietary Fibre 1 g; Cholesterol 140 mg; 2006 kJ (479 Cal)

Stir the yoghurt, lemon rind and vanilla into the egg yolk mixture.

Using a metal spoon, gently fold the egg whites into the mixture.

Simmer the syrup, then remove the cinnamon stick and lemon rind.

MAHALLABIA
(Almond cream pudding)

Preparation time: 15 minutes
  + 1 hour refrigeration
Total cooking time: 40 minutes
Serves 4

500 ml (2 cups) milk
75 g (2½ oz) caster (superfine) sugar
2 tablespoons cornflour (cornstarch)
2 tablespoons ground rice (see Note)
75 g (2½ oz) ground almonds

1 teaspoon rosewater (see Note)
2 tablespoons flower blossom honey
  (see Note)
2 tablespoons shelled pistachios,
  chopped

1 Place the milk and sugar in a saucepan and stir over medium heat until the sugar has dissolved.
2 Combine the cornflour and ground rice with 60 ml (¼ cup) water and mix to a paste. Add to the milk and cook, stirring occasionally, over low heat for 20 minutes. Add the almonds (the mixture will be quite thick) and cook for 15 minutes, then add the rosewater. Spoon into four small shallow dishes and chill for 1 hour. Drizzle with honey and sprinkle with pistachios to serve.

NUTRITION PER SERVE
Protein 9.5 g; Fat 19 g; Carbohydrate 42 g; Dietary Fibre 2.5 g; Cholesterol 17 mg; 1546 kJ (370 Cal)

COOK'S FILE
Note: Rosewater and ground rice are available from health food stores. If flower blossom honey is not available, use normal honey.

Combine the cornflour, ground rice and water, and mix to a paste.

Stir in the ground almonds (the mixture will be quite thick).

Spoon the mixture into four small shallow serving dishes.

HALVAS FOURNO
(Semolina cake)

Preparation time: 30 minutes
+ 45 minutes cooling
Total cooking time: 30 minutes
Makes 12

115 g (4 oz) unsalted butter, softened
125 g (½ cup) caster (superfine) sugar
125 g (1 cup) semolina
110 g (1 cup) ground roasted hazelnuts
2 teaspoons baking powder
3 eggs, lightly beaten
1 tablespoon finely grated orange zest
2 tablespoons orange juice
whipped cream or honey-flavoured
    yoghurt, to serve

Syrup
750 g (3 cups) sugar
4 cinnamon sticks
1 tablespoon orange rind, julienned
80 ml (⅓ cup) lemon juice
125 ml (½ cup) orange blossom water

Topping
60 g (½ cup) slivered almonds
70 g (½ cup) roasted hazelnuts,
    coarsely chopped

1 Preheat the oven to 210°C (415°F/
Gas 6–7). Grease a 23 cm (9 inch)
square baking tin and line the base
with baking paper. Cream the butter
and sugar in a bowl until smooth. Stir
in the semolina, ground hazelnuts
and baking powder. Fold in the eggs,
zest and juice until well combined.
Spoon into the tin, smooth the
surface and bake for 20 minutes, or
until golden and just set. Leave in
the tin to cool.
2 Meanwhile, to make the syrup,
place the sugar and 830 ml (3⅓ cups)
water in a saucepan. Add the
cinnamon sticks and heat gently,
stirring, until the sugar has dissolved.
Increase the heat and boil rapidly
without stirring for 5 minutes. Pour
into a heatproof measuring jug then
return half to the saucepan. Boil for
15–20 minutes, or until thickened
and reduced to about 170 ml (⅔ cup).
Stir in the orange rind.
3 Add the lemon juice and orange
blossom water to the syrup in the
jug. Pour over the cake in the tin.

When absorbed, upturn the cake
onto a large flat plate. Slice into
4 equal strips, then slice each strip
diagonally into 3 diamond-shaped
pieces. Discard the end scraps, but
keep the pieces touching together.
4 To make the topping, combine the
almonds and hazelnuts and scatter
over the cake. Pour the thickened

syrup and orange rind over the
combined nuts and leave to stand for
30 minutes. Transfer the slices to
plates and serve with whipped cream
or honey-flavoured yoghurt.

NUTRITION PER PIECE
Protein 6.5 g; Fat 22 g; Carbohydrate 80 g;
Dietary Fibre 2.5 g; Cholesterol 70 mg;
2247 kJ (537 Cal)

*Fold the eggs, orange rind and orange
juice into the semolina mixture.*

*Add the juice and orange flower water to
the syrup and pour over the cake.*

HONEY AND PINE NUT TART

Preparation time: 25 minutes
+ 15 minutes refrigeration
Total cooking time: 1 hour
Serves 6

Pastry
250 g (2 cups) plain (all-purpose) flour
1½ tablespoons icing (confectioner's)
    sugar
115 g (4 oz) chilled unsalted butter,
    chopped
1 egg, lightly beaten

Filling
235 g (1½ cups) pine nuts
175 g (½ cup) honey
115 g (4 oz) unsalted butter, softened
125 g (½ cup) caster (superfine) sugar
3 eggs, lightly beaten
¼ teaspoon vanilla essence
1 tablespoon almond liqueur
1 teaspoon finely grated lemon rind
1 tablespoon lemon juice
icing (confectioner's) sugar, for dusting
crème fraîche or marscarpone, to serve

1 Preheat the oven to 190°C (375°F/ Gas 5) and place a baking tray on the middle shelf. Grease a 23 cm x 3.5 cm (9 inch x 1½ inch) deep loose-bottomed tart tin. To make the pastry, sift the flour and icing sugar into a large bowl and add the butter. Rub the butter into the flour with your fingertips until it resembles fine breadcrumbs. Make a well in the centre; add the egg and 2 tablespoons cold water. Mix with a flat-bladed knife, using a cutting action, until the mixture comes together in beads.
2 Gather the dough together and lift out onto a lightly floured work surface. Press together into a ball, roll out to a circle 3 mm (about ⅛ inch) thick and invert into the tin. Use a small ball of pastry to press the pastry into the tin, allowing any excess to hang over the sides. Roll a rolling pin over the tin, cutting off any excess pastry. Prick the base all over with a fork and chill for 15 minutes. Cut 3 leaves 4 cm (1½ inch) long from the scraps for decoration. Cover; chill.
3 Line the pastry with baking paper and fill with pie weights or dried

beans. Bake on the heated tray for 10 minutes, then remove.
4 Reduce the oven to 180°C (350°F/ Gas 4). To make the filling, roast the pine nuts on a baking tray in the oven for 3 minutes, or until golden. Heat the honey in a small saucepan until runny. Beat the butter and sugar in a bowl until smooth and pale. Gradually add the eggs, beating well after each addition. Mix in the honey, vanilla, liqueur, lemon rind and juice and a pinch of salt. Stir in the pine nuts, spoon into the pastry case and smooth the surface. Arrange the reserved pastry leaves in the centre.

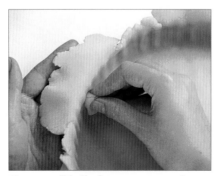

Use a small ball of pastry to press the pastry into the tin.

5 Place on the hot tray and bake for 40 minutes, or until golden and set. Cover the top with foil after 25 minutes. Serve warm or at room temperature, dusted with icing sugar. Serve with crème fraîche or mascarpone.

NUTRITION PER SERVE
Protein 14 g; Fat 63 g; Carbohydrate 83 g; Dietary Fibre 3.5 g; Cholesterol 217 mg; 3936 kJ (940 Cal)

COOK'S FILE
Note: The filling rises and cracks during baking but settles down as the tart cools.

Arrange the reserved pastry leaves over the smoothed pine nut filling.

BAKLAVA
(Middle eastern nut-filled pastry)

Preparation time: 40 minutes
Total cooking time:
   1 hour 20 minutes
Makes 18 pieces

560 g (2¼ cups) caster (superfine)
   sugar
1½ teaspoons lemon zest
90 g (¼ cup) honey
60 ml (¼ cup) lemon juice
2 tablespoons orange blossom water
200 g (7 oz) walnuts, finely chopped
200 g (7 oz) shelled pistachios, finely
   chopped
200 g (7 oz) almonds, finely chopped
2 tablespoons caster (superfine)
   sugar, extra
2 teaspoons ground cinnamon
200 g (7 oz) unsalted butter, melted
375 g (13 oz) filo pastry

1 Place the sugar, lemon zest and 375 ml (1½ cups) water in a saucepan and stir over high heat until the sugar dissolves, then boil for 5 minutes. Reduce the heat to low and simmer for 5 minutes, or until the syrup has thickened slightly and just coats the back of a spoon. Add the honey, lemon juice and orange blossom water and cook for 2 minutes. Remove from the heat and cool completely.
2 Preheat the oven to 170°C (325°F/ Gas 3). Combine the nuts, extra sugar and cinnamon. Grease a 30 cm x 27 cm (12 inch x 11 inch) baking dish with the melted butter. Cover the base with a single layer of filo pastry and brush lightly with the butter, folding in any overhanging edges. Continue to layer the filo, brushing with butter between each new layer and folding in the edges until 10 of the sheets have been used. Keep the rest of the filo under a damp tea towel to prevent it drying out.
3 Sprinkle half the nut mixture over the pastry and pat down evenly. Repeat the layering and buttering of 5 more filo sheets, sprinkle with the rest of the nuts, then layer and butter the remaining filo sheets, brushing the top layer with butter. Press down with your hands so that the pastry

and nuts adhere to each other. Using a large sharp knife, cut into diamond shapes, ensuring you cut through to the bottom layer. Pour any remaining butter evenly over the top and smooth over with your hands. Bake the baklava for 30 minutes. Reduce the heat to 150°C (300°F/Gas 2) and cook for 30 minutes more.
4 Immediately cut through the original diamond markings, then strain the syrup evenly over the top.

Cool completely before lifting the diamonds out onto a serving platter.

NUTRITION PER PIECE
Protein 4.5 g; Fat 23 g; Carbohydrate 40 g; Dietary Fibre 2 g; Cholesterol 28 mg; 1570 kJ (375 Cal)

COOK'S FILE
Note: To achieve the right texture, it is important for the baklava to be piping hot and the syrup cold when you pour the syrup over the top.

Sprinkle the remaining nut mixture over the filo pastry layers.

Strain the cooled syrup evenly over the top of the hot baklava.

ALMOND SEMI FREDDO

Preparation time: 30 minutes
  + 4 hours freezing
Total cooking time: Nil
Serves 8–10

300 ml (10½ fl oz) carton cream
4 eggs, at room temperature,
    separated
85 g (²/3 cup) icing (confectioner's)
    sugar
60 ml (¼ cup) amaretto
80 g (½ cup) blanched almonds,
    toasted and chopped

8 amaretti biscuits, crushed
fresh fruit or extra amaretto, to serve

1 Whip the cream until firm peaks form; cover and refrigerate. Line a 10 cm x 21 cm (4 inch x 8½ inch) loaf tin with plastic wrap so that it overhangs the 2 long sides.
2 Place the egg yolks and icing sugar in a bowl and beat until pale and creamy. Whisk the egg whites in a separate bowl until firm peaks form. Stir the amaretto, almonds and amaretti biscuits into the egg yolk mixture, then carefully fold in the cream and the egg whites until well combined. Carefully spoon into the tin and cover with the overhanging plastic. Freeze for 4 hours, or until frozen but not rock hard. Serve in slices with fresh fruit or a sprinkling of amaretto.

NUTRITION PER SERVE (10)
Protein 5.5 g; Fat 22 g; Carbohydrate 15 g; Dietary Fibre 2 g; Cholesterol 118 mg; 1140 kJ (272 Cal)

COOK'S FILE
Note: Semi freddo means semi-frozen, so if you want to leave it in the freezer overnight, remove it and place it in the refrigerator for 30 minutes to soften slightly before serving.

Place the amaretti biscuits in a plastic bag and crush with a rolling pin.

Beat the egg yolks and sugar together with electric beaters.

Carefully spoon the mixture into the lined loaf tin.

STRAWBERRIES WITH BALSAMIC VINEGAR

Preparation time: 10 minutes
+ 2 hours 30 minutes
marinating
Total cooking time: Nil
Serves 4

750 g (1 lb 10 oz) ripe small
strawberries
60 g (¼ cup) caster (superfine)
sugar

2 tablespoons balsamic vinegar
125 g (½ cup) mascarpone

1 Wipe the strawberries with a clean damp cloth and carefully remove the green stalks. If the strawberries are large, cut each one in half.
2 Place all the strawberries in a large glass bowl, sprinkle the caster sugar evenly over the top and toss gently to coat. Set aside for 2 hours to macerate, then sprinkle the balsamic vinegar over the strawberries. Toss them again, then refrigerate for about 30 minutes.

3 Spoon the strawberries into four glasses, drizzle with the syrup and top with a dollop of mascarpone.

NUTRITION PER SERVE
Protein 6 g; Fat 11 g; Carbohydrate 20 g;
Dietary Fibre 4 g; Cholesterol 30 mg;
830 kJ (200 Cal)

COOK'S FILE
Note: If you leave the strawberries for more than 2 hours, it is best to refrigerate them.
Hint: Thick cream or créme fraîche can be used instead of mascarpone.

Hull the strawberries after wiping clean with a damp cloth.

Sprinkle the caster sugar evenly over the strawberries.

Use good-quality balsamic vinegar to sprinkle over the strawberries.

CASSATA ALLA SICILIANA
(Sicilian ricotta sponge and candied fruit cake)

Preparation time: 25 minutes
+ overnight refrigeration
Total cooking time: 2 minutes
Serves 6

60 g (2¼ oz) blanched almonds, halved
30 g (1 oz) shelled pistachios
650 g (1 lb 7 oz) fresh ricotta cheese (see Note)
60 g (½ cup) icing (confectioner's) sugar
1½ teaspoons vanilla essence
2 teaspoons finely grated lemon zest
50 g (1¾ oz) cedro, chopped into 5 mm (¼ inch) pieces (see Note)
50 g (1¾ oz) glacé orange, chopped into 5 mm (¼ inch) pieces
60 g (2¼ oz) red glacé cherries, halved
375 g (13 oz) ready-made round sponge cake, unfilled
125 ml (½ cup) Madeira or malmsey wine
14 blanched almonds, extra
14 red glacé cherries, extra, halved
icing (confectioner's) sugar, for dusting
sweetened whipped cream, to serve

1 Dry-fry the almonds and pistachios in a frying pan, tossing, over medium heat for 2 minutes, or until starting to change colour. Cool.
2 Press the ricotta through a sieve over a bowl. Stir in the icing sugar, vanilla, lemon zest, cedro, glacé orange, glacé cherries and nuts. Mix.
3 Grease a 1.25 litre (5 cup) pudding basin. Cut the cake horizontally into 1 cm (½ inch) thick slices. Set aside one round and cut the rest into wedges, trimming the base to make triangles. Sprinkle the cut side of the triangles lightly with Madeira and arrange around the base and side of the bowl, cut-side down, trimming if necessary to fit. Spoon the ricotta mixture into the centre. Top with a layer of cake. Press down firmly and neaten the edges. Chill overnight.
4 Carefully unmould onto a serving plate. Arrange the extra almonds and cherries on top and dust with icing sugar just before serving. Serve with sweetened whipped cream—piped into patterns for a true Sicilian look.

NUTRITION PER SERVE
Protein 17 g; Fat 53 g; Carbohydrate 63 g; Dietary Fibre 3 g; Cholesterol 132 mg; 3328 kJ (795 Cal)

COOK'S FILE
Note: It is important to use fresh ricotta from the deli so it can be moulded successfully.
Cedro is candied citron peel and is available from most Italian delicatessens. If unavailable, use glacé pineapple and ½ teaspoon finely grated lemon zest.

Arrange the pieces of sponge cake around the base and side of the basin.

Spoon the ricotta mixture into the cake-lined pudding basin.

Top with a layer of sponge cake, press down firmly and neaten any edges.

INDEX

INTERNATIONAL GLOSSARY OF INGREDIENTS

capsicum	red or green pepper	tomato paste (Aus.)	tomato purée, double concentrate (UK)
chilli	chili pepper, chile		
eggplant	aubergine	tomato purée (Aus.)	sieved crushed tomatoes/ passata (UK)
fresh coriander	fresh cilantro		

This edition published in 2008 by Bay Books, an imprint of Murdoch Books Pty Limited. Pier 8/9, 23 Hickson Road, Millers Point, NSW 2000, Australia.

Managing Editor: Rachel Carter **Editors:** Anna Sanders, Wendy Stephen **Food Director:** Jane Lawson **Food Editor:** Rebecca Clancy **Creative Director:** Marylouise Brammer **Designer:** Norman Baptista **Recipe Development:** Alison Adams, Rebecca Clancy, Judy Clarke, Ross Dobson, Michele Earl, Jo Glynn, Katy Holder, Jane Lawson, Valli Little, Kate Murdoch, Angela Tregonning **Home Economists:** Renee Aiken, Ross Dobson, Justin Finlay, Valli Little, Kate Murdoch, Angela Tregonning, Wendy Quisumbing **Nutritionist:** Thérèse Abbey **Photographers:** Ian Hofstetter, Reg Morrison (steps) **Food Stylist:** Marie Hélène Clauzon **Food Preparation:** Justine Poole, Valli Little **UK Consultant:** Maggi Altham **Chief Executive:** Juliet Rogers **Publisher:** Kay Scarlett

The nutritional information provided for each recipe does not include garnishes or accompaniments, such as rice, unless they are included in specific quantities in the ingredients. The values are approximations and can be affected by biological and seasonal variations in food, the unknown composition of some manufactured foods and uncertainty in the dietary database. Nutrient data given are derived primarily from the NUTTAB95 database produced by the Australian New Zealand Food Authority.

ISBN 978 0 681 01347 6
Printed by Hang Tai Printing Company Limited. PRINTED IN CHINA.
Reprinted 2008.